HEARTBROKEN

HEARTBROKEN

GRIEF AND HOPE INSIDE THE OPIOID CRISIS

ELLEN KROHNE

WITH MATTHEW ELLIS, MPE
& DIANA CUDDEBACK, LCSW

Paperback ISBN: 978-1-7332983-0-8
eBook ISBN: 978-0-578-54177-8

Cover and Interior Design: Creative Publishing Book Design

Printed in the United States of America

To the seven brave parents who lay bare their hearts as a way to give a voice of hope for healing to all of those struggling with addiction and to the families that love them.

In loving memory of all the families who have lost a loved one to the opioid crisis.

Table of Contents

Part III: The Opioid Crisis - Conclusions

Acknowledgements

So many people came into my life as this book evolved. I am so grateful you did! My co-authors, Matt and Diana, I appreciate that you pushed and pulled to make our words about the opioid crisis both purposeful and meaningful. I believe we all feel like **Heartbroken** is our baby, and she wouldn't have been possible without you. I'll be forever grateful.

Sincere thanks to our Book Angels, David, Debby, Donna, Dorothy, Joy and Kate who read the early drafts and provided us with their insightful comments and suggestions.

Brad Stetson, content editor, provided us needed perspective, and helped form and mold the book. Kathy Mueller served as expert copy editor and proofreader. Ghislain Viau, with Creative Publishing Design, did the cover design and formatting. The Hauser Group is working with us on marketing the book. We so appreciate all of their expertise and dedication to this project.

Special thanks to Mid-America Transplant Foundation for connecting me with one of the families and providing information on organ donation. Kristen Shinn with Hoyleton Youth and Family

Services, and Dennis Trask with the Southern Illinois Substance Abuse Alliance, provided much-needed expertise in prevention strategies.

Thank you to my son, Ab, for his assistance with visuals and for sharing his experience in the book; to my daughter, Joy, for her input and encouragement; and to my husband, Bill, for his ever-present support.

And, finally, thanks to the seven brave parents and families that each offer you, dear reader, their intimate story of the opioid epidemic and how it changed their family forever. They will always be in my heart.

A Word to the Reader
By Ellen Krohne

I have to admit that, prior to this endeavor, I had not thought much about the opioid crisis. It had not impacted me personally. Of course, the news reports of so many people dying bothered me. It seemed to be getting worse every year, and I had little understanding as to why. One of my high school classmates lost his grandson to a drug overdose. I couldn't imagine how hard that must be.

In January 2018, I went to a "Ladies' Night Out" that was sponsored by the Washington County Health Department in my small community, Okawville, Illinois. The speakers presented on the impact of the opioid crisis in Washington County, Illinois, a rural and very community-oriented county of only 14,000 people. They shared statistics of drug use and addiction deaths that were astonishing. There were 15 drug-related deaths in this county in the last five years, eight of which were from opioid overdoses, and three specifically from heroin. Prior to 2013, there were almost no overdose deaths. I went home in shock that my little part of the world was so heavily impacted. How did I not know that?

This book was written so that we will all know.

Later that week, I met with Diana Cuddeback, the Director of Heartlinks Grief Center. I knew that, a year earlier, Heartlinks had started a new grief group meant just for families that had lost loved ones to drug addiction, the "Addiction Loss Support Group." Diana wasn't shocked by my revelations on the drug crisis. She confirmed that it was bad and getting worse - everywhere. Not just here in Illinois, but all across the United States.

I asked her if there were resources about coping with this crisis that I could read. She knew of a couple of resources, but said that there really isn't much available for those grieving from an addiction loss. I started doing a little digging. There was a lot of information about the opioid crisis and heroin, many written with opinions on who's to blame. There were books full of facts that were almost unbelievable on how this crisis was impacting people all across the United States. However, I could only find a few helpful stories about how families at the heart of the crisis managed, living with addiction day-to-day. There was little regarding specific actions that we could all take to make a difference in turning it around. And very little about how to help families cope with their grief from the loss of a child to drug addiction.

Over the next few months I continued my research and reflected a lot on the opioid crisis, and on what I had been learning. My neighbor's grandson, Zach, asked me, "Are you working on another book?" Last year I was blessed to have written my first book, **We Lost Her**, which told the story of my family's grief journey after our mom died tragically in 1970. I told Zach that I had the stirrings of a book, about families that had journeyed through the opioid crisis and lost a loved one, but that I was overwhelmed by the data and the expertise I'd need to write on this topic.

I believe God puts in our path those whom we need, when we need them, and what Zach said next was evidence of this. He said, "I have a friend whose Ph.D. dissertation and field of expertise is the opioid crisis – would you like me to introduce you to him?"

"Yes," I said, "Absolutely." Zach's friend is Matthew Ellis, MPE (Masters of Psychiatric Epidemiology.) I pored over his published research, and Matthew and I met at a coffee shop in St. Louis soon afterwards. I was excited when he agreed to be a co-author, providing the expertise which I lacked in this subject. He is based in St. Louis at Washington University's School of Medicine, in the Department of Psychiatry. I was just as elated that Heartlinks Grief Center's Director, Diana Cuddeback, LCSW (Licensed Clinical Social Worker) agreed to provide her grief counseling expertise and experience, and also be a co-author to this work. Diana is the founder of Heartlinks Grief Center, and also brings extensive trauma-related grief experience.

Diana offered to let me speak with the attendees of the Addiction Loss Support Group, and ask if any of them would like to participate in telling their story for a book on the opioid crisis. With both of them onboard, *Heartbroken: Grief and Hope Inside the Opioid Crisis* was born.

Most of the families that you will read about in the chapters ahead are members of the Heartlinks Addiction Loss Support Group. One of them came to this work through the Mid-America Transplant Foundation. All of these stories are heartbreaking. And that's about all they have in common.

The stories are, in fact, strikingly different. Different regarding how their children started using opioids - from a soldier suffering with PTSD, to an adolescent having his wisdom teeth removed. Different regarding how they received treatment, or weren't able to access it, or didn't accept treatment. They range from families that struggled on high alert for a decade, to one that did not have any knowledge of their child's drug use. Some children were from large families, while others were the only child. Some parents practiced "tough love," and others just couldn't.

The children who were lost were not teenagers experimenting with drugs. The average age at death was 27 years old, which, I have learned, is a typical age for overdose deaths.

All of the divergent stories have the same sad ending. As you will read, these families tried everything to help their children, all with different courses of action, and all were courageous in the face of the unthinkable. And each of the families is now coping in a different way with the aftermath, their grief, and the work of putting their lives back together again.

One piece of feedback that I received from my first book, **We Lost Her**, is that I should have written a warning to the reader to have a box of Kleenex at hand when reading it. I'll put that warning right here. The stories are sad, indeed.

Although sad, it is imperative for them to be told, to be understood. The families who agreed to share their journeys through the nightmare of a child's drug addiction and death, did so because they want to help others, to allow others insight into what really happens to a family in the throes of this crisis. We, the authors, want to put a face to this crisis and give it a voice. We are hopeful the information and data accompanying these stories will be a call to action for each of us to stop the stigma associated with addiction and loss, and to help stem this crisis.

And, maybe, just maybe, it will help keep a child and a family from having to endure this experience.

And, maybe, just maybe, it will enable hearts to become open to those struggling with addiction, and with grief from addiction loss.

I had a myriad of emotions as I absorbed and wrote the families' stories of loss: sadness, shock, anger. The one thought I had over and over as I listened to each family's pain was, "There but for the grace of God go I." These children struggling with addiction were from caring families and had parents that were concerned for them. You know, like you and I, dear reader, they had dinner together and read to them when they were little. They protected and disciplined them and reveled in their children's achievements. The children had doting grandparents and loving extended families. None of that protected them. Every child is vulnerable to drug addiction. Please don't hold the families in these stories at arm's length, but take them into your hearts.

My co-authors and I are humbled to tell the families' stories, and hope that in doing so we've honored the life that was lost, and the lives left to live with their pain. I thank the families for their courage in sharing the stories. And I thank you for the courage to read them, the commitment to take action in order to motivate changes that will help bring an end to the crisis, and for the compassion to find ways to help those who are grieving their loved ones lost to this crisis.

———— // ————

This book is organized as follows:

In **Part One, Chapter One**, Matthew walks us through, in plain terms, how we in the United States got to this place in the opioid crisis. In **Chapter Two**, Diana introduces concepts about grief and how we perceive it, particularly grief from addiction loss.

In **Part Two, Chapters Three through Nine**, Seven Families' Journeys Through Drug Addiction - Loss of a Child and Grief, I, Ellen, put a voice and a face to the stories of these families. One parent from each family met with me for an interview, and this is the person whose voice is used in the story that I wrote afterwards. The families then provided me with their feedback and, after a few drafts, approved their story. This process was, in every case, very emotional and heart-wrenching for them. But they love their children so much that they want to tell their stories to help others. Each story is written in the tone and voice in which their personal journey was related to me.

Every one of the parents in the stories is a brave person. As you read, you will come to understand that, just like you and I, they are not perfect. Some of the choices they made and examples they set may seem less than ideal. The parents live with the consequences of those decisions. "Regret points" is what one mother called them. We can see them with clarity now, in hindsight. Just like parents everywhere who are struggling to raise their children, they did their best.

Two of the families have chosen not to use their real names. One has an active police investigation still underway. The other family felt that the death is just too recent. The remaining four stories are written as a memoir, and include special photographs and memories of their lost loved one. I've indicated which ones are anonymous at the start of the chapter.

Each story has two parts. The first part contains the journey of the family through their child's addiction and death. The second part describes how the family is managing their grief.

Chapter Seven has an addition that reflects a special part of that family's story: a Q&A on organ and tissue donation, provided by Mid-America Transplant.

At the end of each chapter, Diana Cuddeback provides **Grief Reflections**, insights and take-aways from the real-life story. She outlines what we can learn from each story about grief, and some actions we can take to help those who are grieving from an addiction loss.

There is one family who just couldn't put their story into print in this book. The mother said, "In writing, it is just too devastating. My other daughters just cannot bear it." She did agree to a very short version of the important learnings from her experience, which is **Chapter Nine** of **Part Two**.

Part Three, The Opioid Crisis - Conclusions, wraps up the book.

In **Chapter Ten,** Matthew Ellis outlines the specifics we have learned from the families' stories about the opioid crisis, the role that stigma plays in this crisis, and some specific actions we can each take to make a difference in helping to end this crisis. He also describes both policy change imperatives, and needed changes to current treatment options.

In **Chapter Eleven,** I describe education and prevention strategies that are currently being employed, and provide resources and suggestions for what each of us can do to prevent a loved one, particularly a child, from starting down the path of substance use.

Chapter Twelve includes closing thoughts from Diana and, finally, from me.

In the **Appendix** you will find reference information and resources which we hope will help you to learn more about opioids, addiction and loss, and what you can do to help stem the crisis. One of the Appendices contains a listing of opioid drugs, and definitions of many of the terms used throughout the book. The questionnaire which I used in the interviews with the families, a resource list, and discussion guides are also included here.

You will notice that each of the three authors writes in his or her own style, and we've not tried to change that. Matthew's sources are cited at the end of Chapter One and Chapter Ten, while Diana and I refer to our information sources within the text in our chapters.

This book, like *We Lost Her*, has another purpose: to provide funds for Heartlinks Grief Center, which is a part of Family Hospice of Belleville, Illinois, a 501(c)3, not-for-profit organization. Heartlinks Grief Center provides grief counseling, both to individuals and in groups, to those in Southern Illinois, regardless of ability to pay. Profits from the sales of this book will help provide funding for the Center. I am grateful to volunteer with Heartlinks Grief Center, and to serve on the Family Hospice Board of Directors, and I am grateful to you, dear reader, for purchasing this book and helping to provide funding for them.

Here's how to connect with the authors:

- Ellen Krohne – www.ellenkrohne.com
- Diana Cuddeback – www.myheartlinks.com
- Matthew Ellis – ellism@wustl.edu

Part I

The Opioid Crisis and Grief – an Introduction

In Chapter One, Matthew explains, in plain terms, how we in the United States got to this point in the opioid crisis. In Chapter Two, Diana introduces concepts about grief and how we perceive it, particularly grief from addiction loss.

Paved with Good Intentions – A Brief History of the Opioid Epidemic

By Matthew Ellis, MPE

The story of the current opioid epidemic in the United States is a contradiction of sorts. It is simultaneously the unique result of several factors colliding at once, as well as the same old story that has existed throughout countless centuries for any number of substances used to alter the mind and body. While we have yet to reach, or even to see, the ending of this story, the havoc already wrought is something that has not been seen in the United States outside of military action. In 2017, the United States recorded its all-time highest number of opioid overdose fatalities, with more than 47,600 of the 70,237 drug overdose deaths attributed to opioids[1]. Despite two decades of opioid research, policy, intervention, prevention and education, the opioid overdose rate has not declined, nor even leveled off. In fact, the past few years have seen the greatest year-on-year increases of opioid overdose fatalities. Americans are now more likely to die from an opioid overdose than from a car accident[2]. How did we get to this point?

———— // ————

Wave I: The Prescription Opioid Epidemic

In 1980, the New England Journal of Medicine, arguably the most prestigious medical journal in the country, published a curious bit of correspondence from a physician who, in reviewing 11,882 patients taking at least one narcotic, determined that only four of these met the criteria for "reasonably well-documented addiction. [3]" This led him to title his letter with the conclusion, "Addiction is rare in patients treated with narcotics [opioids]." Since this letter was published in the "Correspondence" section of the journal, it did not undergo the typical peer-review process that is the norm when publishing scientific research. That did not stop it, however, from being frequently cited by other healthcare providers, professional organizations and, notably, pharmaceutical companies, throughout the 1980s and 1990s as justification for the expansion of opioid utilization.

Prior to this time period, opioids were a class of drug not frequently prescribed. However, those pharmaceutical manufacturers and professional organizations which focused on pain began shifting the norms of the medical community by branding opioids as a safe and effective treatment option for a condition that many saw as an undertreated epidemic: chronic, non-cancer pain.

This conversation surrounding opioids and chronic pain came to a head in 2000, when the Joint Commission on Accreditation of Healthcare Organizations noted that chronic pain was a serious epidemic, that it afflicted tens of millions of Americans, and that it was vastly undertreated by the healthcare profession. It not only advocated pain as the "fifth vital sign," meaning that pain should be routinely assessed by physicians, but also that there existed an underutilized class of drugs that could help alleviate this epidemic: opioids[4, 5].

As it happened, during this same time period, the pharmaceutical industry was transforming the idling opioid market by introducing a new type of opioid, extended-release opioids. The first and most popular of these was OxyContin. Prior to this, the vast majority of prescription opioids was "immediate-release," meaning that the drug was delivered to the body's system upon ingestion. As such, only a small amount of the drug was included as part of a pill/tablet, and the rest of the tablet was filled with another substance, primarily acetaminophen or ibuprofen. For patients, particularly older ones, this meant having to remember to take pills, keeping careful track of them, every few hours.

To mitigate this requirement, and to make it easier for patients, a new opioid formulation was designed to be taken only once or twice a day. Extended-release opioids would release the opioid drug slowly into one's system over a long period of time. However, in order to achieve this, the additional substances were removed, and more of the opioid was packed into a single pill. In fact, these extended-release drugs were initially marketed as, "less abuseable" because if patients ingested them, they would not get the instantaneous rush of the immediate-release opioids[6, 7]. In actuality, the opposite occurred.

It was quickly discovered, and broadcast across the budding internet, that these pills were easily crushed or dissolved for snorting or injecting, and that by doing so, you could defeat the extended-release mechanism and ingest the large amount of opioid in a single pill at one time[6, 8-11]. When subsequent actions by certain pharmaceutical companies included covering up abuse information, aggressive marketing, and other inappropriate business practices[12, 13], other pharmaceutical companies followed suit, and the niche opioid market exploded into one of the biggest drug markets ever seen.

In hindsight, the advent of extended-release opioids and the emphasis on undertreated chronic pain became the "big bang" of the opioid epidemic. Prescriptions for opioid medications skyrocketed in the United States, and while other countries saw only moderate increases in the prescription and subsequent abuse of these drugs, the United States became one of the world's leading consumers of opioids[14]. In 1997, opioids were prescribed at a rate of 96 mg per person, but by 2007 this rate had increased to 700 mg per person[15]. For OxyContin, prescriptions grew from 670,000 in 1997 to 6.2 million in 2002[7]. It is often asked, why these drugs? Why were prescription opioids the drug that took off across America? What was unique about the opioid experience in the United States that was not found in other countries?

First, prescription opioids were perceived as safer than other drugs[16]. Although opioids can provide the user with a sense of euphoria, these were drugs that went through testing and approval processes with the Food and Drug Administration, and were deemed safe to release to the public. They were prescribed by physicians, whom patients usually trusted, and upon whose professional decisions they typically relied. They were used for many conditions and were consumed by people of all ages. If they posed a particular threat, one would think that this would not be the case, so people perceived them as "safe." Dosages, in particular, were right there on the pill, so there was no question of what you were getting. And finally, this form of drug abuse was more socially acceptable because it carried much less of the stigma that was associated with other drugs of addiction.

Second, there was a proliferation of opioids flooding the market. Pharmaceutical companies both met and increased the demand by an explosion of new opioid classes, new formulations, varying dosage strengths, etc. Opioids became a first line of defense for both acute and chronic pain. However, physicians received little education on pain management, and even less on prescribing opioids appropriately[17, 18]. In particular, prescription opioids were, and still are, a primary form of treatment for physicians and health systems in rural areas that are not as resource-rich as the urban areas[19, 20], which typically contain large university partners. This, coupled with aggressive marketing to both physicians and consumers, created a ripe market for the mass distribution of prescription opioids, both legal and illegal[21, 22].

A third, often overlooked but critical, component of the opioid epidemic is the purpose that these drugs served for individuals *outside* of their therapeutic use. For many individuals addicted to opioids, the pathway begins by first discovering the benefits of these drugs while taking them as prescribed[23, 24]. This develops into their use outside of what is directed by the prescription or the physicians. Eventually, as tolerance builds, a pattern of problematic use emerges and culminates in an opioid addiction. Treatment may be sought, or the opioids may continue to be used to simply avoid withdrawal sickness, or to provide some ability to merely function on a day-to-day basis.

However, in those initial stages, prescription opioids are described as filling a variety of needs for individuals. Most common are escaping from life stressors (e.g., losing a job, going through a divorce), coping with past trauma (e.g., abuse, the death of a loved one), seeking productivity, or self-treating psychological issues (e.g., depression, anxiety)[23]. Psychological discomfort or prior psychiatric diagnoses - mental health issues - are the most notable, as nearly three-fourths of opioid users who sought treatment reported a prior history of such issues[25-31].

As shown in the graph below, produced by the Centers for Disease Control and Prevention (CDC), from 1999-2010 the culmination of these factors resulted in large increases in treatment admission for opioid use disorder, as well as large increases in opioid overdose fatalities, both of which rose in tandem with increases in the sales and distribution of these medications[32].

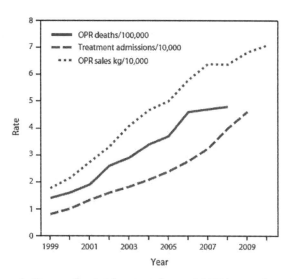

Figure 1. Rates of opioid pain reliever (OPR) overdose death, OPR treatment admissions, and kilograms of OPR sold — United States, 1999—2010[32]

As the prescription opioid epidemic expanded across the United States, the response from policymakers was focused on only one side of the issue. Starting in the early 2000s, interventions and policies were put into place in order to stifle the prescription and subsequent diversion of prescription opioids. Put more simply, these were interventions focusing on the "supply" side of prescription opioids. Lawmakers put in place legislation restricting "pill mills" and high-volume pain clinics that acted as a revolving door for opioid-seeking patients[33-36].

Prescription Drug Monitoring Programs (PDMPs) were established in every state (except Missouri) in order to keep track of patient prescriptions from multiple sites, thus providing a roadblock to doctor shopping[37-39]. For physicians, increased attention and education was centered on prescribing patterns, patient risk, and dosage amounts. The CDC added prescribing guidelines in 2016, which continue to remain a topic of controversy among healthcare providers, due to concerns about reverting back to a system that undertreats patients in need[40].

Finally, pharmaceutical companies introduced abuse-deterrent formulations of opioids, with the goal of making opioids harder to crush or dissolve, in order to prevent users from snorting or injecting these drugs.[41-43].

There has been much debate about the impact of these efforts to restrict opioids for those who use these medications for therapeutic reasons and, counter to that, about whether opioids are effective in long-term patient care. Regardless, overall these supply-side efforts have led to a reduction in overall prescriptions in the United States, as shown in the graph below[44], and there is now evidence that this has reduced the magnitude of the prescription opioid epidemic[45].

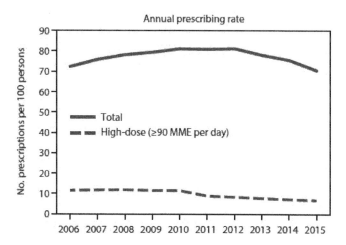

*Figure 2. Annual opioid prescribing rates per 100 persons —
United States, 2006–2015[44]*

The prescription opioid epidemic did, however, open the door for many users to another type of opioid, an illicit one that does not go through a testing process, have a dosage amount on it, or provide any clue about its true contents: heroin.

Wave II: The Rise of Heroin

While the United States was focusing most of its energy on tackling prescription opioids, heroin began to creep in under the radar. The second wave of the opioid epidemic was a "perfect storm" resulting from three intertwining factors.

First, for many users, addiction is a process. While not universal, one of the most common patterns of abuse progresses from swallowing and chewing pills, to smoking or snorting them, and finally to injecting them. As tolerance builds with the sustained use of opioids, users need to take more pills at once, or move to stronger opioids (e.g., heroin), or find more immediate ways to introduce opioids into their system (e.g., injection). It is important to note, however, that for many users, once a certain level of tolerance has been reached, use is no longer about getting high. The use of opioids, whether illicit or the prescription variety, simply serves to maintain the individual's normal functioning[16]. Without them, withdrawal sickness will set in and, more often than not, drugs are sought after to stave off these horrific symptoms. The euphoria of these drugs becomes either non-existent, or found only in the relief from the symptoms of withdrawal.

Second, the focus on reducing both the legal and illegal supply of opioids had significant effects for the existing population of prescription opioid users. As prescription opioids were prescribed less frequently, patients on long-term opioid care were cut off, and several popular prescription opioids were also reformulated to be abuse-deterrent, so some opioid users shifted to heroin[46]. Not only were prescription opioids harder to find, but when they were available, market forces had raised their prices, leading users to seek an alternative that was more cost-effective. But cost was not the only driving factor. Those who had progressed in their use of opioids could not revert back to using low-potency varieties. Therefore, a suitable substitute needed to be found.

Although it was an unintended consequence, heroin readily filled the gaps left by the reduced supply of prescription opioids. It is important to note that the proportion of those who use prescription opioids and subsequently use heroin is small, estimated at less than 5%. However, even though this number is small, the risks are greater, which is why the overdose rates have continued to increase despite a smaller group of people using these high-risk opioids[47]. The focus on supply-side efforts, while an important component in mitigating the opioid epidemic, has failed to get to the root cause of the opioid epidemic or, put more succinctly, we continue to ignore the demand side of the substance abuse equation.

As noted above, in the early stages of use, opioids fulfill a number of needs for their users, i.e., to self-treat mental health issues, escape from life, or cope with stress. And until a greater focus is placed on these issues, we will merely be treating the symptoms of addiction rather than the disease.

Finally, the heroin market has drastically changed in recent years in response to the increased use of, and demand for, the drug[48]. For much of the past few decades, heroin was primarily sourced from Asia. But as demand grew in the United States, Latin American countries began to take on more of the production and distribution, and have since supplanted Asia as the leading source of heroin in the United States. This meant that heroin became more readily accessible, cheaper, and had consistently higher purity than ever before in the United States.

As heroin grew in popularity, production in Latin America was ramped up to meet the increased demand, and heroin became more widely distributed across the US. This had several effects on drug markets:

1) The demographics of heroin users changed from popula-tions of inner-city minorities, who were often (and unjustly) ignored, to populations more closely aligned with the prescription opioid epidemic: predominantly white commu-nities in rural or suburban areas[49].

2) The stigma of heroin as a drug only used by "junkies" began to recede, as it became more widely used and more socially acceptable[49]. And,

3) The use of heroin as a recreational drug became more popular, with research now showing that more and more individuals are bypassing prescription drugs as their initiation to opioids, and starting their opioid use with heroin[50].

This latter point is the most serious issue so far, because naïve users can easily overdose on a single use of heroin. This is because they have no tolerance to opioids, they don't know the purity of the heroin, there is the potential that the heroin contains other substances (e.g., fentanyl), and they have little experience in how to separate and administer an appropriate dosage. Heroin does not come in a manufactured pill with a trusted dosage amount printed on it.

While evidence was showing a "bend in the curve" of prescription opioid use, the above intertwined factors led to increased heroin use, with the result that opioid fatalities began their largest year-on-year increases in 2010. But before the country could get its bearings on how to handle this new heroin epidemic, an even greater threat emerged: the proliferation of illicitly manufactured fentanyl.

Wave III: A New Opioid Epidemic – Fentanyl

Prescription fentanyl is a synthetic opioid which is 50 to 100 times more powerful than morphine, the standard opioid against which other opioids are measured, and is most often used in managing pain from cancer, or in end-of-life care. However, black market drug producers found a way to develop fentanyl very cheaply, and as the heroin market was expanding in the United States, they sought to capitalize on the illicit opioid trend.

Interestingly, this fentanyl epidemic can almost be viewed as a separate opioid epidemic. Its supply was coming from a different source, primarily China[51], and its introduction into the illicit drug market was covert, not one that was actively sought out.

Fentanyl is often mixed with heroin, but it is also produced as counterfeit pills. A number of overdose deaths have been reported when counterfeit pills, that were thought by their users to be hydrocodone, oxycodone or benzodiazepines, turned out to actually be fentanyl[52-54]. Many substance users mentioned their fear that their drugs might contain fentanyl, suggesting that the demand side of fentanyl use is different from the demand that had been seen for prescription opioids and heroin[55, 56].

All of the heroin risks noted above are multiplied significantly for fentanyl, which carries a potency that is higher than heroin and most prescription opioids. One milligram of fentanyl is equivalent to 100 milligrams of morphine. To put that in context, one milligram of OxyContin is equivalent to one- and one-half milligrams of morphine.

While overdoses were notably increasing as a result of the heroin expansion, the magnitude of that increase was still small compared to what happened after fentanyl flooded the United States. As shown in the graph below, fatalities from illicitly manufactured fentanyl now dwarf those from prescription opioids and heroin[57].

While this overview is just a brief synthesis of the opioid epidemic, and does not include a comprehensive discussion of some of the many other factors that played a role, such as distributors and pharmacists, diversion channels, geographic variation, etc., the point is that from 1999 to 2017, almost 400,000 individuals died

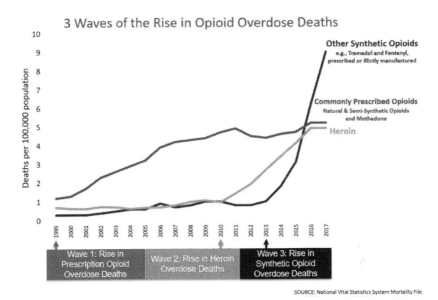

Figure 3. 3 Waves of the Rise in Opioid Overdose Deaths [57]

from an opioid overdose[1]. The epidemic has grown to the extent that the life expectancy in the United States dropped in 2017 for the first time since World War II[58].

While so many individuals have lost their lives to this terrible epidemic, what should not be forgotten is that every one of those 400,000 individuals left behind people they loved, people they cared about, and people who loved them. An often-unrecognized secondary effect of these tragedies is that there are millions and millions of people who have lost somebody to opioid addiction. Millions of individuals who have grieved, millions of individuals who try to understand, millions of individuals who will never see their parent, their spouse, their friend or their child again. It is time that their voices are heard.

Endnotes

1. Scholl, L., et al., *Drug and Opioid-Involved Overdose Deaths - United States, 2013-2017*. MMWR Morb Mortal Wkly Rep, 2018. **67**(5152): p. 1419-1427.

2. Council., N.S. *Injury Facts*. Available from: *https://injuryfacts.nsc.org/all-injuries/preventable-death-overview/odds-of-dying/*.

3. Porter, J. and H. Jick, *Addiction rare in patients treated with narcotics*. N Engl J Med, 1980. **302**(2): p. 123.

4. Baker, D., *The Joint Commission's Pain Standards: Origins and Evolution*. Division of Healthcare Quality Evaluation, 2017. **The Joint Commission**.

5. JN, C., *APS 1995 presidential address*. Pain Forum, 1996. **1**(5): p. 85-88.

6. Office, U.S.G.A., *Prescription Drugs: OxyContin Abuse and Diversion and Efforts to Address the Problem*. GAO-04-110, 2003.

7. Van Zee, A., *The promotion and marketing of oxycontin: commercial triumph, public health tragedy*. Am J Public Health, 2009. **99**(2): p. 221-7.

8. Cone, E.J., et al., *Oxycodone involvement in drug abuse deaths: a DAWN-based classification scheme applied to an oxycodone postmortem database containing over 1000 cases*. J Anal Toxicol, 2003. **27**(2): p. 57-67; discussion 67.

9. Carise, D., et al., *Prescription OxyContin abuse among patients entering addiction treatment*. Am J Psychiatry, 2007. **164**(11): p. 1750-6.

10. Hays, L.R., *A profile of OxyContin addiction*. J Addict Dis, 2004. **23**(4): p. 1-9.

11. Hadland, S.E., et al., *Association of Pharmaceutical Industry Marketing of Opioid Products With Mortality From Opioid-Related Overdoses*. JAMA Netw Open, 2019. **2**(1): p. e186007.

12. Ryan, H., Girion L, Glover S, *'You Want a Descripiton of Hell?' OxyContin's 12-hour Problem*, in *Los Angeles Times*. May 5, 2016.

13. Emanuel, G., Thomas, K, *Top Executives of Insys, an Opioid Company, Are Found Guilty of Racketeering*, in *The New York Times*. May 2, 2019.

14. Board, I.N.C., *Narcotic Drugs-Technical Report*. Estimated World Requirements for 2019: Statistics for 2017., 2019. **United Nations**.

15. Paulozzi LJ, B.G., Franklin GM, et al. , *CDC Grand Rounds: Prescription Drug Overdoses-a U.S. Epidemic.* . MMWR Morb Mortal Wkly Rep, 2012. **61**(1): p. 10-13.

16. Cicero, T.J. and M.S. Ellis, *The prescription opioid epidemic: a review of qualitative studies on the progression from initial use to abuse.* Dialogues Clin Neurosci, 2017. **19**(3): p. 259-269.

17. Davis, C.S. and D. Carr, *Physician continuing education to reduce opioid misuse, abuse, and overdose: Many opportunities, few requirements.* Drug Alcohol Depend, 2016. **163**: p. 100-7.

18. Schnell, M. and J. Currie, *Addressing the Opioid Epidemic: Is There a Role for Physician Education?* Am J Health Econ, 2018. **4**(3): p. 383-410.

19. Weinhold, I. and S. Gurtner, *Understanding shortages of sufficient health care in rural areas.* Health Policy, 2014. **118**(2): p. 201-14.

20. McGrail, M.R., et al., *Measuring the attractiveness of rural communities in accounting for differences of rural primary care workforce supply.* Rural Remote Health, 2017. **17**(2): p. 3925.

21. Dunn, K.E., et al., *Opioid Overdose Experience, Risk Behaviors, and Knowledge in Drug Users from a Rural versus an Urban Setting.* J Subst Abuse Treat, 2016. **71**: p. 1-7.

22. Monnat, S.M. and K.K. Rigg, *Examining Rural/Urban Differences in Prescription Opioid Misuse Among US Adolescents.* J Rural Health, 2016. **32**(2): p. 204-18.

23. Cicero, T.J. and M.S. Ellis, *Understanding the demand side of the prescription opioid epidemic: Does the initial source of opioids matter?* Drug Alcohol Depend, 2017. **173 Suppl 1**: p. S4-S10.

24. Srivastava, A.B. and M.S. Gold, *Beyond Supply: How We Must Tackle the Opioid Epidemic.* Mayo Clin Proc, 2018. **93**(3): p. 269-272.

25. Bohnert, A.S.B. and M.A. Ilgen, *Understanding Links among Opioid Use, Overdose, and Suicide.* N Engl J Med, 2019. **380**(1): p. 71-79.

26. Edlund, M.J., et al., *Opioid abuse and depression in adolescents: Results from the National Survey on Drug Use and Health.* Drug Alcohol Depend, 2015. **152**: p. 131-8.

27. Fink, D.S., et al., *Patterns of major depression and nonmedical use of prescription opioids in the United States.* Drug Alcohol Depend, 2015. **153**: p. 258-64.

28. Katz, C., et al., *Risk factors for incident nonmedical prescription opioid use and abuse and dependence: results from a longitudinal nationally representative sample.* Drug Alcohol Depend, 2013. **132**(1-2): p. 107-13.

29. Kaye, A.D., et al., *Prescription Opioid Abuse in Chronic Pain: An Updated Review of Opioid Abuse Predictors and Strategies to Curb Opioid Abuse: Part 1.* Pain Physician, 2017. **20**(2S): p. S93-S109.

30. Seal, K.H., et al., *Association of mental health disorders with prescription opioids and high-risk opioid use in US veterans of Iraq and Afghanistan.* JAMA, 2012. **307**(9): p. 940-7.

31. Webster, L.R., *Risk Factors for Opioid-Use Disorder and Overdose.* Anesth Analg, 2017. **125**(5): p. 1741-1748.

32. Paulozzi LJ, J., CM, Mack, KA, Rudd RA., *Vital Signs: Overdoses of Prescription Opioid Pain Relievers — United STates, 1999--2008.* MMWR Morb Mortal Wkly Rep, 2011. **60**(43): p. 1487-1492.

33. Johnson, H., et al., *Decline in drug overdose deaths after state policy changes - Florida, 2010-2012.* MMWR Morb Mortal Wkly Rep, 2014. **63**(26): p. 569-74.

34. Kennedy-Hendricks, A., et al., *Opioid Overdose Deaths and Florida's Crackdown on Pill Mills.* Am J Public Health, 2016. **106**(2): p. 291-7.

35. Lyapustina, T., et al., *Effect of a "pill mill" law on opioid prescribing and utilization: The case of Texas.* Drug Alcohol Depend, 2016. **159**: p. 190-7.

36. Surratt, H.L., et al., *Reductions in prescription opioid diversion following recent legislative interventions in Florida.* Pharmacoepidemiol Drug Saf, 2014. **23**(3): p. 314-20.

37. Chang, H.Y., et al., *Impact of prescription drug monitoring programs and pill mill laws on high-risk opioid prescribers: A comparative interrupted time series analysis.* Drug Alcohol Depend, 2016. **165**: p. 1-8.

38. Fink, D.S., et al., *Association Between Prescription Drug Monitoring Programs and Nonfatal and Fatal Drug Overdoses: A Systematic Review.* Ann Intern Med, 2018. **168**(11): p. 783-790.

39. Finley, E.P., et al., *Evaluating the impact of prescription drug monitoring program implementation: a scoping review.* BMC Health Serv Res, 2017. **17**(1): p. 420.

40. Dowell, D., T.M. Haegerich, and R. Chou, *CDC Guideline for Prescribing Opioids for Chronic Pain--United States, 2016.* JAMA, 2016. **315**(15): p. 1624-45.

41. Litman, R.S., O.H. Pagan, and T.J. Cicero, *Abuse-deterrent Opioid Formulations.* Anesthesiology, 2018. **128**(5): p. 1015-1026.

42. Lee, Y.H., D.L. Brown, and H.Y. Chen, *Current Impact and Application of Abuse-Deterrent Opioid Formulations in Clinical Practice.* Pain Physician, 2017. **20**(7): p. E1003-E1023.

43. Dart, R.C., et al., *Do abuse deterrent opioid formulations work?* J Opioid Manag, 2017. **13**(6): p. 365-378.

44. Guy, G.P., Jr., et al., *Vital Signs: Changes in Opioid Prescribing in the United States, 2006-2015.* MMWR Morb Mortal Wkly Rep, 2017. **66**(26): p. 697-704.

45. Dart, R.C., S.G. Severtson, and B. Bucher-Bartelson, *Trends in opioid analgesic abuse and mortality in the United States.* N Engl J Med, 2015. **372**(16): p. 1573-4.

46. Cicero, T.J. and M.S. Ellis, *Abuse-Deterrent Formulations and the Prescription Opioid Abuse Epidemic in the United States: Lessons Learned From OxyContin.* JAMA Psychiatry, 2015. **72**(5): p. 424-30.

47. Compton, W.M., C.M. Jones, and G.T. Baldwin, *Relationship between Nonmedical Prescription-Opioid Use and Heroin Use.* N Engl J Med, 2016. **374**(2): p. 154-63.

48. Ciccarone, D., G.J. Unick, and A. Kraus, *Impact of South American heroin on the US heroin market 1993-2004.* Int J Drug Policy, 2009. **20**(5): p. 392-401.

49. Cicero, T.J., et al., *The changing face of heroin use in the United States: a retrospective analysis of the past 50 years.* JAMA Psychiatry, 2014. **71**(7): p. 821-6.

50. Cicero, T.J., M.S. Ellis, and Z.A. Kasper, *Increased use of heroin as an initiating opioid of abuse.* Addict Behav, 2017. **74**: p. 63-66.

51. O'Connor, S., *Fentanyl Flows from China: An Update since 2017.* Issue Brief, November 26, 2018. **U.S.-China Economic and Security Review Commission**.

52. Lucyk, S.N. and L.S. Nelson, *Novel Synthetic Opioids: An Opioid Epidemic Within an Opioid Epidemic.* Ann Emerg Med, 2017. **69**(1): p. 91-93.

53. Coopman, V., et al., *A case of acute intoxication due to combined use of fentanyl and 3,4-dichloro-N-[2-(dimethylamino)cyclohexyl]-N-methylbenzamide (U-47700)*. Forensic Sci Int, 2016. **266**: p. 68-72.

54. Administration, D.E., *DEA Issues Nationwide Alert on Fentanyl as Threat to Health and Public Safety*. https://www.dea.gov/divisions/hq/2015/hq031815.shtml., 2015

55. Ciccarone, D., J. Ondocsin, and S.G. Mars, *Heroin uncertainties: Exploring users' perceptions of fentanyl-adulterated and -substituted 'heroin'*. Int J Drug Policy, 2017. **46**: p. 146-155.

56. Mars, S.G., D. Rosenblum, and D. Ciccarone, *Illicit fentanyls in the opioid street market: desired or imposed?* Addiction, 2018.

57. Prevention, C.f.D.C.a., *Opioid Overdose: Understanding the Epidemic*. https://www.cdc.gov/drugoverdose/epidemic/index.html, 2019.

58. Murphy, S.L., et al., *Mortality in the United States, 2017*. NCHS Data Brief, 2018(328): p. 1-8.

CHAPTER TWO

Navigating the Grief of Addiction Loss

Diana Cuddeback, LCSW

Grief Process

Renowned grief theorist Therese Rando gave this definition of grief: *Grief refers to the process of experiencing the psychological, behavioral, social, and physical reactions to the perception of loss.* Grief is a universal experience; if you can love and be attached, you can grieve. But grief looks different for each person and for each relationship. It is like drawing a cat. If 10 different people draw a cat, each picture will look different, but there will be enough similarity that anyone can see that each picture is a cat. Grief is like that; we know what it is, but a firm and clear definition is difficult and very individualized.

Grief is a nonlinear process that doesn't fit well into discreet stages. You meander in and out of grief, back through and around.

You end up dealing with the same thoughts and feelings over and over in a prismatic way, turning the glass and seeing the reflections from slightly different perspectives. Grief is a life-long trip. Most people who grieve explain that they don't want "closure." Closure is an idea discussed by media and therapists, but not grievers. Grievers don't want their thoughts, feelings and memories closed off. They want to remember, but without overwhelming pain.

Each story in this book illustrates a part of the grief process that is helpful to understand. Without giving you theories and too much academic-sounding talk, the authors of this book and the people who have shared their stories hope to give the reader concrete ideas, direction, and a sense of community with others who are sharing a similar journey of loss.

Before we introduce the story portion of this book, there are a few more things to know about the grief that is related to addiction loss, things that often set this grief apart from other types of loss. It's essential to understand ideas such as stigma, disenfranchised grief, and traumatic grief.

Stigma and Disenfranchised Grief

The Addiction Loss Support Group at Heartlinks Grief Center, which I direct, came into existence because parents attending the Child Loss Support Group after an addiction-related loss were not comfortable sharing fully. These parents were worried about the **stigma** surrounding addiction. Stigma is typically described as a mark of disgrace associated with a particular circumstance, quality, or person. People in the general child-loss group were kind. No one said anything hurtful. But parents and siblings who had navigated addiction before their loss had stories and memories to share that they felt uncomfortable sharing with people who had not also navigated those difficult experiences.

Addiction-loss parents wanted to talk about years of hiding anything of value, and sleeping with their wallet under their pillow, in a group where others understood. They wanted to share about the relief of knowing the phone would not ring with horrible news, now that their child had died. And they wanted to say that they would live through all of the craziness again if their child could just be alive. Saying this in a room full of people who had lost children to accidents or illness felt uncomfortable, because those grieving parents had no context for understanding it.

The stigma of addiction separates and isolates. Weathering these experiences makes one sensitive to judgment for oneself and for the person who died due to their addiction. No one wants to chance the risk of judgment of their child or themselves. This puts people grieving a loss due to addiction in a very uncomfortable place. That uncomfortable place, that stigma, isolates and separates people dealing with addiction.

This discomfort from stigma can be explained by a well-known concept. Grief after an addiction-related loss can be considered **disenfranchised grief**. This term was developed by grief researcher, Ken Doka, about two decades ago. He defines disenfranchised grief as:

"Grief that persons experience when they incur a loss that is not or cannot be openly acknowledged, socially sanctioned or publicly mourned."

Doka suggests that this can happen for a variety of reasons that tend to fall into one or more of the following categories:

1. The loss isn't seen as worthy of grief (like a non-death loss, such as divorce)

23

2. The relationship is stigmatized (for example, when the partner in an extramarital affair dies)

3. The mechanism of death is stigmatized (like a suicide or overdose death)

4. The person grieving is not recognized as a griever (for example, when an ex-spouse dies)

5. The way someone is grieving is stigmatized (like when a grief response seems extreme, or when someone shows no outward grief responses)

When someone dies of addiction, their loss may be mourned publicly, but there is often blame and fault attached to their death. These are generally directed at the decedent, and sometimes at his or her family. Early in the opioid crisis it was unusual to see a clear cause of death mentioned in an obituary of a young person who had not been ill. People were left to guess, question and talk. What happened? Did they die by suicide? Questions and gossip often abounded. As the epidemic has gone on, people are acknowledging the cause of death more often. Obituaries are often full of clear warnings or poignant stories of a life lost to substance use. This blame and faulting add to the disenfranchising grief after an addiction-related loss. Understanding addiction is one key to helping people advocate for their grief experience, and reduce the stigma surrounding this sort of loss. If you reduce the stigma, you stop the disenfranchisement.

The disease model of addiction has been acknowledged by the American Medical Association since 1956. Recently, research has been providing an increasing understanding of the brain-disease model of addiction. Still, as you will read in the stories to follow, there is a sense of blame and guilt associated with an addict. There is a subtle and less-than-subtle assertion that, because of addiction, a death was expected, and that the dead person was at fault because addiction was their "choice." Several people experienced comments that expressed a dismissal of the death because the addicted individual was at fault. Other stories portray the belief that an addict is less worthy of regard, and even medical care, than a non-addict. All of these instances show why an addiction loss can result in disenfranchised grief.

Trauma

For your final consideration, as you get ready to read the individual stories of addiction-related loss, be aware that the process of living with addiction, both as an addict and as someone caring for an addicted person, may leave individuals with trauma. **Trauma** is the response to a deeply distressing or disturbing event that overwhelms an individual's ability to cope, causes feelings of helplessness, and diminishes both the sense of self and the ability to feel the full range of emotions and experiences. It is a clinical term that has a clear set of diagnostic standards. The scope of this book is less to give a clinical picture, and more to inform the reader as a starting place for healing. We won't go deeply into diagnostic criteria and explanations.

Do consider that if you have lived with the extreme ups and downs, and the life-and-death situations of an addicted love one, that your body has experienced chronic trauma. Your autonomic nervous system and its fight-or-flight emergency-response function has had a regular workout in navigating relapses, safety concerns, legal issues, midnight calls, "tough-love" interventions, and overdoses. Your emergency system may be sort of stuck in an "on" position after intense and/or prolonged use of that emergency-response mode.

This factor can complicate the grief process. But there are specific and effective interventions to manage trauma responses. It is beyond the scope of this book to be a comprehensive trauma work, but you will find basic education, a few tangible interventions, and additional resources to get you started in managing this typical aspect of addiction-related loss.

Part II

Seven Families' Journeys Through Drug Addiction

———//———

In Part Two, Seven Families' Journeys Through Drug Addiction - Loss of a Child and Grief, I, Ellen, put a voice and a face to each family's story. These stories have two parts. First, the journey of the family through their child's addiction and death is told. The second part of the story describes how the family is managing their grief.

At the end of each chapter, Diana Cuddeback provides Grief Reflections, insights and takeaways from the real-life story. She outlines what we can learn from each story about grief, and some actions we can take to help those who are grieving from an addiction loss.

CHAPTER THREE

A Tale of Two Ryans

By Ellen Krohne

This is Ryan's story, as told by his mother, Ann.

Diana Cuddeback, the Director of Heartlinks Grief Center, invited me to the monthly Addiction Loss Support Group in September, 2018. My purpose in attending was to talk about my plan to write a book about drug addiction and grief, and to see if any of the group's participants would be willing to share their story. I sat next to Diana, and on my other side sat a woman younger than me. Ann introduced herself and shook my hand. I liked her immediately.

Ann had a radiant smile, and I could feel her strength. I wondered whom she had lost, and what her story was. Diana had told me that she was a good "adapter" of the techniques they discussed: breathing exercises, meditation, and journaling. Ann was using her new techniques and was open to trying any suggestion as she journeyed through her grief.

After I spoke to the group, Ann was the first one to say, "I'm in – I want to tell my son's story." I was so grateful she had volunteered.

When we met a few weeks later to talk about her son's story, I still had this comfortable feeling about her. I didn't realize her grief was so recent, or just how strong she really is.

———⸗———

"I don't have any family that lives here. My parents are long gone, and my only half-brother died from drugs in the '80's. He was 45 and I was 30. I saw how drugs and alcohol affected my brother's life, and how much it hurt my mom. Back then, his alcohol and drug use were considered a lifestyle choice, not a disease or an addiction. I didn't want that for my life. Even though my brother had addiction problems, I was still so naïve about drugs and addiction, what the symptoms were and what to look for. I had no idea. It's easy to look back now and know just what to undo.

We are just normal people, my husband and I. I am an accountant. Greg is an electrician. We got married in 1977 and decided we wanted three children – no reason for three, just that it sounded right for us. Then my first pregnancy ended in a miscarriage, as well as my second and third. We finally had a little boy, Ryan, on September 8, 1990. He was born six weeks premature, but grew and thrived. We were thrilled to have him, our son, finally! A few years and miscarriages later, we realized he'd be our only child.

Ryan was a smart child – and I say that not just because he was mine. His teachers and everyone else said he was brilliant. When he was three years old, the preschool teachers asked me, "How did you teach him to read?"

I said, "I didn't teach him. I thought you did." Turns out he taught himself. I read to him all the time from when he was a baby on, and he just picked it up. He wanted me to read the Encyclopedias to him when he was in kindergarten.

I asked him, "Well, what part do you want me to read?"

He said, "Just start with the A's, Mom."

He loved books. He was that kid that was happiest at the library. Or playing a practical joke. He had this dry wit. I found it so entertaining. He'd play elaborate practical jokes on me. When he was twelve, we started letting him stay home alone for short periods between when Greg left for his shift work and I got home. One day I got home and couldn't find him. Screaming frantically for him through the house, I got to my bedroom and there were legs sticking out from under the bed. Of course, Ryan was hiding behind the door dying of laughter as I screamed. There was always a gift with a spider or snake that popped out at Christmas. I still have some of them on my shelves, just so I can remember his sense of humor.

Ryan enjoyed writing stories, poems and music. He loved playing the guitar. Other people's feelings were important to my caring boy. He just had a gentle way about him. Ryan decided as a young teen that killing animals so that we could eat them was wrong. He was a vegetarian from that day forward. He had that kind of resolve.

He grew into a very tall, (6 ft. 4 inches), lanky young man with this beautiful, brown hair and twinkling blue eyes. His eyes were how I could tell whether he was using drugs or not. They always gave him away. That, and he looked unkempt when he was using. When he wasn't using, he cared about his appearance.

Ryan's drug abuse journey started very innocently when he was 15. We took him to have his wisdom teeth cut out, and the doctor sent us home with a bottle of pills. Opioids. I didn't know what it was. The doctor said to give them to him for pain, so I did. Ryan told me years later that he LOVED the feeling they gave him. He didn't tell us that then. But when the pills were gone, he found he could buy them at high school. And he did. He didn't tell us that, either.

The pills were expensive, though, and when he found he could get the same feeling, the same high, from heroin, which was much cheaper, he started using that. He told us years later he didn't feel he had a choice by then to use or not, he felt he had to have it.

We thought his erratic sleeping was just normal teenage behavior. We never suspected he was a drug addict. He was 17 when we found out.

We got a call from the police on September 30, 2007 to tell us that Ryan had overdosed in a park. What? I couldn't take in what they were saying. The two friends he was with tried to help him walk it off in a nearby woods but, luckily, a nurse at the park saw that Ryan was convulsing and called 911. Of course, the friends took off. The police said to come to the park immediately, and then we met them at Belleville Memorial. The nurse at Memorial asked if we wanted a priest to come, because Ryan might not make it to Cardinal Glennon. I called our priest, who said, "I am too busy to come." I was hurt and done with that priest. It would be the last time I would ask him for anything. Ryan was immediately airlifted to Cardinal Glennon in St. Louis. When we got there and saw him, we were in shock.

His eyes were bugged out – he couldn't even see us. I thought, "I should take a picture so he can see what he has done to himself." Then I couldn't take it, scared it may be his last photo and I didn't want that. They warned us he might not make it and, if he did, he could have brain damage.

I stayed the night with him, in disbelief that he'd used drugs. We didn't know what he'd taken. We'd find out later about his addiction.

The next morning, he just sat up in bed and was fine. "Hi Mom," he said.

Later we learned that what he had taken the day before in the park was acid. We learned that our son was a heroin addict, and had been for some time. We were so upset and just in shock. We knew we had to get him help, get him into rehab, immediately.

We sent him to Gateway Rehab, a facility near our home. Outpatient counseling, two to three evenings a week for several months. We'd taken away his car privileges, so I drove him and waited. The counselor said he was doing great. Then, unexpectedly, he just went downhill fast. It was the start of his senior year and he went from straight "A's" to flunking his classes. He had a fabulous SAT score and could have gone to any college, but his grades the last year of high school kept him out of most schools.

He went back to rehab a couple more times over the next year. He kept having what we'd come to call "slip-ups." Slip-ups were him going back to heroin. Ryan would tell me when he was clean for a while that heroin would tempt him. He'd say, "I think I can do a little bit, just one time, I have this under control." And of course, he didn't. It would lead to a slip-up.

He started seeing a wonderful young woman, Ceara, in late 2009. She was going to school in St. Louis at St. Louis University. When her roommate graduated, she moved in with us for a little while until she and Ryan could get an apartment.

She wasn't a drug user and didn't tolerate him using drugs, either. He loved her enough to want to be clean. They moved in together and he was doing great. They had a cute apartment that she decorated, and a cat they loved. He was on a good path, we thought.

In 2013, Ryan started on Suboxone and seemed to be doing well. Suboxone works to end the cravings and helps with the withdrawal pain. Suboxone helped him to stay off of illegal opioids, like heroin. In 2014 he started decreasing his dose to wean himself off of the Suboxone, per his doctor's orders. The doctor should have given him a plan for reducing the dosage and some type of counseling. I wish he could have stayed on it forever. Suboxone is very expensive, and when he turned 26 he would no longer be on our insurance, and he was worried about how he would be able to afford it for the rest of his life.

He ended up with another slip-up and went back to rehab. This time they gave him Naltrexone, a narcotic antagonist. This drug works by blocking the effects of opiate drugs in the brain, too, and if you use opioids while taking Naltrexone, it has very severe side effects, sending the user into immediate withdrawal.

One day in June of 2015, Ceara called us, hysterical. She was rushing Ryan to a local hospital near their apartment. She suspected that he had used heroin and she confronted him. He wanted to prove to her that he hadn't (when he had, of course and wasn't thinking rationally) so he took his Naltrexone to prove it to her, and was having a horrific reaction – shaking, convulsing. He was a mess.

Ceara got him quickly to the Emergency Room. As she rushed Ryan in, the staff was horrible in their treatment of him, the nurse calling him, "scum of the earth," and yelling at him to hold still when his legs were trembling. He couldn't control himself.

After the episode with the Naltrexone, we realized that Ryan needed more than the usual outpatient rehab. We'd been in contact with Chad Sabora, who ran the Missouri Network for Opiate Reform and Recovery. His organization holds Narcotics Anonymous meetings. His help was a lifeline for us.

Chad Sabora got Ryan into a rehab facility in Florida. He was able to get him in right away, and it was far enough away that he could not leave easily. He was inpatient this time, and then was sent to a halfway house. No contact with us or Ceara for six weeks, while he was in rehab or the halfway house, from June till October, 2015. Ceara had stood by him and we were hopeful that this would be the rehab that would truly turn his life around.

Ryan broke up with Ceara while he was still in Florida, and he also tried to push Greg and me away. Later he told me that he never quit loving Ceara, but he couldn't keep hurting her. He came back from Florida in December of 2015, doing very well, and we were hopeful that this one would stick. When he came back, he started seeing Ceara again, as a friend. It didn't take long and they were back together, but it didn't last long. Ceara broke up with Ryan in April. She didn't feel that she could trust him to stay away from drugs and she was too stressed.

Ryan and Ceara had been together for over five years when he had the Naltrexone episode. Ryan had had only a couple of "slip-ups" during those years, but we'd always get him into rehab as quickly as we could, locally to Gateway or Chestnut.

Ryan was effectively two different people. One was our wonderful Ryan, our sincere, caring, funny, smart son. The other was Heroin Ryan. Heroin Ryan was not our Ryan. It was heroin that took over Ryan's body. He was sloppy, irrational, a liar. Heroin

Ryan would do anything to get his drugs. And when Heroin Ryan showed up, we did what we had to do – we did the "tough love."

When Heroin Ryan was present, if he didn't agree to rehab, we wouldn't let him stay with us. We would push him out of our house and lock the door. We just had to hold on. Usually, the threat of our "tough love" would make him go back to rehab. It was hard, but "tough love" was the right thing for us. It took every bit of strength I had, as his mother, to kick him out, but Greg and I both knew we had to, or we'd lose him to his drug.

One time we locked him out and the cops picked him up. They kept him overnight, but let him out the next day. They didn't even press charges against him. It seems amazing to me that he had all these years of drug use and he was never incarcerated.

He'd screw up, slip up, and we'd be able to pull him back. He never got to the point of no return, where he was so far gone that he couldn't come back. I'm so grateful for that. It kept him with us for nine years after we found out he was an addict. I'm grateful to have had him for those years, addict or not.

His world was rocked when Ceara came down with cancer, lymphoma, not long after he returned, and they broke up. Ryan felt that he had caused her cancer, with all the stress his drug use brought to their relationship. He tried to keep some distance from her, trying not to upset her anymore, but keeping track of how she was doing by talking to other people. He told me he didn't want to hurt her anymore. While Ceara did recover from cancer, their relationship never did. They never got back together.

Ryan had been out of the Florida rehab for about a year, living with us again, when one of the counselors he met in the Florida rehab center, Chelsea, called and asked him to move to Portland, Oregon with her. Chelsea was also a recovering addict who had been clean for five years. But instead of going to Oregon, she showed up at our doorstep in August of 2016. Ryan asked if she could move into our house, along with the German Shepard puppy she had brought with her. We had an uneasy feeling about them together, but if it made Ryan happy and helped him stay clean, we'd give it a try. She got a job. It was his birthday September 8th, and he was doing so well that we celebrated with him for the whole month. He loved going to all of his favorite restaurants every year during his birthday month: Indian, pizza, cheesecake. I'll always treasure those dinners with him.

One October night, Ryan and Chelsea didn't come home from a night of partying in St. Louis. A limo pulled up to our house the next morning, and out fell Chelsea. "Where's Ryan?" she screamed at us, not making any sense. We finally came to understand that they'd done some drugs and Ryan took Chelsea to the Emergency Room at Barnes Hospital in St. Louis when she overdosed. Ryan must have been out of control, too, and when a cop came and threatened to cuff Ryan to a bench, he fled. Chelsea was released the next morning, but didn't have any idea where Ryan had gone. He called us about four hours later. He'd had a flat tire on Chelsea's car in St. Louis somewhere. We went to get him.

Time for more "tough love." We told Ryan, "Back to rehab or get kicked out." We called Chelsea's mom in Florida. Ryan and Chelsea didn't agree to rehab. They both quit their jobs, loaded everything into her car and moved in with someone in St. Louis. They didn't let us know where they were, because they knew we would call the police. At the end of November, Ryan called, pleading for help. He promised to go to rehab, and that Chelsea's dad would come and get her. I went over to get them and collected their things from an abandoned house in the city – the most awful conditions you can imagine. I couldn't believe my son was there.

Chelsea's dad came and got her car and sent her to a rehab in Oregon. Ryan was on a long waiting list to get into a rehab in Chicago, so he stayed home with us. He was 26 by now.

While he was waiting, in December 2016, Ryan found a program that seemed to give him hope, direction, and purpose for his life. It was Launch Code, a nine-month class in St. Louis that trains people for jobs in computer coding. He was excited and did great in the classes. He found a job as a cook at Freida's Deli, near the school. It was a vegan restaurant and he fit in perfectly.

He talked about his future, something he'd not done for years. He told me, "I want to get my degree in Philosophy, be a professor, open a book store that would also sell local artists work. I want Chelsea and I to have a life together." He described it as what he and Ceara had before, a small place that she would decorate, and they would have a cat. "I know what I want, Mom," he said.

And he seemed to have really changed! He'd turned a corner. Before, he hid his drug use, never wanting anyone except close friends to know. When he was going to Launch Code and working at Freida's, he told everyone he was a recovering addict. He wanted everyone to be "watching out" for him, so he didn't slip up again. He trimmed his hair and dressed as the preppy, hoping he wouldn't be approached by drug dealers. These months, as he studied and worked, he was our Ryan again. He was doing so well, and we hoped that our roller coaster ride was finally over.

On Thursday, February 16, 2017, Ryan was excited for the upcoming weekend. I went to bed about ten. Ryan was home and came into our bedroom, wanting to borrow my Netflix controller, as he couldn't find his. He gave me a goodnight kiss and went downstairs. He lived in a separate apartment on the lower level of our home. He had his own kitchen and entrance; it was nice for him and for us.

Greg came home from work around 11 p.m. that night and, as he always did, came in through the downstairs to say hi to Ryan. That night, it was all quiet. He found Ryan in the bathroom with a needle in his leg. He yelled for me and started CPR. I called 9-1-1. I think that Greg was thinking, as I did, "Here we go again." Not thinking that this was the end – not now.

The paramedic arrived and she was wonderful. She had been to our home before for Ryan's overdoses. They tried Narcan, but it didn't work. Ryan had a heartbeat when the paramedics got there. They took him to Belleville Memorial Hospital, the same place our nightmare with drugs started. Greg and I followed, frantic that they couldn't revive him. He'd overdosed so many times, we knew the drill – but this felt different.

They put Greg and I in a room. It took what seemed like forever for someone to come. A doctor finally came into the room and told us that Ryan was dead. I have no memory of the words she said, just that I knew he was dead. I remember screaming. I couldn't believe it. I still can't. Someone asked me if I needed a wheelchair. I didn't want one, I just wanted to get to him. A minister that works with addicts came and sat for hours with us. He was very comforting.

There is so much I don't remember about the hours after we learned that Ryan was dead. And the next days and weeks. I think my mind protects me from what I just can't bear to remember. I'm thankful for that.

We learned weeks later that what Ryan took was not heroin, it was Fentanyl. He didn't have any heroin in his system, just the Fentanyl. Narcan doesn't work as effectively on Fentanyl, as it would need to be administered quickly and in several doses. I don't think Ryan went out to buy Fentanyl; his drug of choice was heroin. I learned that dealers sell their users Fentanyl, because it's synthetic and cheaper to make than heroin. Dealers don't care that it's so dangerous that just a little can cause an overdose and death. Dealers have so many buyers that one less doesn't matter to them. I guess especially one that hadn't bought for a while.

The coroner didn't release his body for almost a week. The police were trying to find the dealer that had sold him the heroin. He'd have gotten the death penalty if they had convicted him. But they never did arrest anyone.

The day after Ryan died, our house was filled with friends and relatives. Good friends that Greg and I will always love. Feeding us, writing Ryan's obituary, being there for us, not leaving us alone. Greg's niece took us to the funeral home to make the arrangements.

I just couldn't function – I could barely breathe. My chest felt like it was caving in, like I'd been shot, like there was a hole in me. Someone called a doctor, but my friends wouldn't let me take the pills the doctor sent. There was no pill for this pain.

We decided to have Ryan cremated. Then we thought about all of his friends who just couldn't believe he was gone. Most of his close friends knew of his addiction and his being clean for a few months. They, too, were in shock that he was gone. We decided, for them more than for us, to have him laid out at a visitation before the cremation.

I'm glad we did. So many of them came to his "Celebration of Life." We had pictures and a touching slide show of his life which Greg's niece had put together. Ryan's good friend, Sean, created a CD that alternated a song that Ryan wrote and performed with a song by a performer that Ryan really liked. The CD played at Ryan's Celebration of Life. It was comforting, to see all the people there that loved him. We didn't have a mass or a service. Ryan wasn't religious. So many people posted their love for him on Ryan's Facebook page. Sean also put together some of the posts into this poem. It sums up our son's life well:

> You are calm truth
> We would all crank our necks
> To stare up at you
> But you never once
> Looked down on us
> One of the most brilliant
> People I have ever met
> Your songs, your jokes
> Your sincerity, your love
> I can't imagine a world
> Without them
> But there won't be one
> Your songs will be played
> Your jokes will be told
> Your sincerity will be shared
> And your love will be felt forever
> By all of us lucky to have witnessed
> Your beauty."

———— // ————

Ann didn't cry as she told me Ryan's story. She came close a couple of times, but she took a deep breath and I could see her settling herself. She showed me a necklace which she fingered as we finished talking. It had Ryan's thumbprint on one side and this saying on the other: "Ryan, loving intelligent gentle son. My treasure."

Ann continued, sharing her grief journey with me.

———//———

"I just don't recall most of the first year after he died. After his funeral service, it seemed to get harder every day. I couldn't go out of the house. Just couldn't make myself get up and walk out the door. I had this hole in my heart and it wasn't healing. No one could see it, but I felt the pain every moment.

I decided, about six months after we lost him, to get braces on my teeth. I figured I hurt so much anyway, now would be a good time to get that done.

My friends tried to help. They were always there for us. Some sent me links on the internet with suggestions on grief or books to read. One book that was helpful to me was **Option B** by Sheryl Sandburg. Other friends called, came by, tried to be there for me. But none of them understood this pain or really knew how to help. None of them had been through a traumatic loss.

"Take as much time as you need," my boss told me. He offered to let me work from home if that would help. They were just wonderful. A person I worked with, Cheryl, came by to visit. I knew her, but we weren't close. I consider her a close friend now. She'd lost her Mom in a tragic house fire a few years earlier. She started coming by the house. She gently nudged me to get out of the house.

She told me, "You need to get back to work. Don't worry, I'll talk to the bosses and co-workers who do not know what happened, so you don't have to tell them."

She saved me.

She was right. Going back to work gave me something to focus on other than the pain. It was stressful, though, and I got shingles soon after I went back. Some at work were surprised that Ryan had died of an overdose, saying things like, "Why did he do drugs, why didn't he just quit?" My mama bear instinct would rear up, feeling the need to defend Ryan even now, and I'd ask them, "Why do you still smoke? Addiction is just that – you can't just quit once you're addicted."

Some, including family, said hateful, mean things about drug addicts. One said, "The only people that deserve to die are drug addicts." I almost came across the table at that one, but decided to control myself, as it wouldn't do any good. Some people just don't get that drug addiction could happen to their kids, just like it happened to Ryan.

Others just wanted to know how they could help, which was heartwarming. I told them, "Just talk about Ryan, don't try to pretend it didn't happen. You won't make me cry; I just cry sometimes anyway. I want to talk about him going forward." He was my son and always will be. Talking about him is the best thing to help heal this hole in my heart.

On the first Mother's Day after Ryan died, Cheryl called me and asked, "What are you doing on Mother's Day?"

I told her, "I don't have any plans; Greg is working."

She said, "You are coming with me, we are going on the boat for the day." She made sure the day was spent relaxing and enjoying the lake. And talking about Ryan. She helped me tremendously.

The other thing that helped me was finding Heartlinks Grief Center Addiction Loss Support Group. One of Ryan's counselors at Gateway Rehab called and suggested I attend. I started attending the Addiction Loss Support Group in March, 2017. I thought that after the first year, the hole in my heart would heal and it would get easier. It didn't. It seems even harder this year.

The Addiction Loss Support Group saved me, too. Finding people to talk with that understood what I'd been through felt amazing. Being the parent of an addict is so crazy. Greg and I were always on edge, just waiting for slip-ups, waiting for Heroin Ryan to emerge, wondering what was next on the roller coaster. It's hard to come down from that constant state of worry, the constant state of high alert. I was worried every time the phone rang that it was some new bad news about Ryan.

But the people at the support group had all been there, too. They had experienced the same horrors of living with and losing their child to drugs. I could talk freely about Ryan without judgment at the support group. I could even laugh there, almost feel normal again. I can't even say how much the group helps me, and means to me.

Diana, the Heartlinks Director, leads the group. She taught us breathing exercises and meditation. I practice every night and it's allowed me to sleep again. Before, I'd be on "high alert," like I was all those years before Ryan died. Practicing meditation has allowed me to sleep, and my blood pressure is down, too.

Greg tried coming with me to the Heartlinks Addiction Loss Support Group, but he wasn't as comfortable sharing with the group. It's not for everyone. Greg talks to the guys at work. We don't say a whole lot to each other, as we don't want to bring each other down. We talk about the good times. He had in his heart that Ryan wasn't going to make it, that the Heroin Ryan would take him down. I guess I thought our "tough love" and getting Ryan into rehab would always work, that he'd always come back.

Now that I've lived through Ryan's addiction and death, I realize what's really important in life. What's important are relationships, and since I don't have family nearby, my friends are what matters. If it was God who got me through this hell, He worked through friends and people who cared about me. So, people come first. If anyone asks me to do something now, I'm open. I realize they may not be there the next weekend. So, I say yes.

I think the best way to help someone that's lost a loved one is to acknowledge and remember the person they lost. To talk about the person, share memories, say their name, not try to pretend they never lived, never died.

Back when I was growing up, kids experimented with drugs and most didn't end up dead. They smoked pot or did speed, but most didn't end up addicted for life. But that's what today's drugs do – one use of prescription opioids or heroin, and some are down a path of no return. It just doesn't seem right that drugs which are so addictive are legal, and prescribed to children.

I hate it so much when people say, "My kid would never do that." Judgmental, inferring Ryan was not a good person. We did everything we could to save Ryan, once we realized he was addicted. But it was too late. They just don't realize how easily addiction happens. All kids are at risk – one time using drugs and they could end up addicted.

Ryan would often tell me, "It wasn't my choice, it's not what I want. I loved the way the pills made me feel and didn't realize it was so bad. By the time I realized, it was too late."

Ryan wrote me several letters. I think he wrote this one in 2015 or 2016, and I'll always cherish that he knew how much I believed in him and loved him.

Dear Mom:

First and foremost, I would like to let you know how much I love you, how much I appreciate all that you have done for my own betterment. Granted, I have not always behaved in a manner which is indicative of such a love and appreciation. I have on occasion (sometimes on a frequent) occasion acted selfishly, showing little regard for the feelings of others.

This was especially true in my treatment of those who love me most (namely you, dad, and Ceara). In making my decisions, I would oftentimes disregard others in favor of furthering my own interests, or at least my own interests as I falsely interpreted them to be.

All the while, though, you never lost sight of my *real* interests, my *best* interests. My actions would stand in stark opposition to my professed life goals. This fact was easily lost on me. It was never lost on you. You consistently stood by my side, refusing to let hope go. Even when I hurt you most, you were willing to forgive and forget so that I could move forward with my life.

Accordingly, I have two main goals in writing you this letter. First off, I want to apologize once again for all the pain and worry I have put you through over the years. Finally, I would like to thank you once more for all that you have done for me.

You always told me that I would one day recognize your actions as being in my best interests, as being made from a place of love. I think that day may have arrived.

Love,

Ryan

P.S.—Almost everything said in this letter is also applicable to dad.

The thing that I think we as a nation should change, in order to stop this horrible crisis of losing people to drug addiction, is to never prescribe an opioid to a minor. Their minds are still developing and they are not able to know what these drugs will do to their lives. We need to come up with something for pain that's not addictive.

I miss Ryan's hugs, his kindness, playing a game or having a conversation with him. I still talk to him; he just doesn't talk back. He was such a good conversationalist. We'd argue and he'd give good points and opinions. I miss that the most.

We still have the German Shepard puppy that Chelsea showed up with at our door. Ryan loved that pup. He keeps us entertained.

The only word to describe the journey we have traveled, and are still on, is "horrible." We've decided to put Ryan's ashes in a bulb where a tree will grow out of them. I just can't take him out of our china cabinet yet. I'm feeling strong, but I'm just not strong enough yet."

Ryan in 2009   *Ryan in 2016 before his death*

A Tale of Two Ryans
– Grief Reflections –
By Diana Cuddeback, LCSW

Grieving the loss of anyone is demanding. Grieving the loss of your child is unimaginable. Ryan's story is full of ideas for people grieving after a death. It also holds ideas for people who are dealing with the daily grief of living with a loved one who is battling an addiction. These stories share examples of grief that include loss of trust, loss of a sense of safety and predictability, of relationship, of the hopes and dreams that parents have for their children, or that people who love one another have for each other. This portion of the book will draw the reader's attention to the ideas included in each chapter for managing loss, and ideas for helping with grief.

Grief before and after a loss is overwhelming and impacts the physical, social, emotional, spiritual and psychological parts of us as humans. Everything changes. What we believed about people and how the world is ordered, as well as how we assumed the world works, can feel lost. **Finding a focus and routine** can bring you comfort and keep you upright. Ann talks about her return to work as giving her a focus other than the pain. She had support around her for that return - people who gave her time off and people who supported her movement back into the work environment.

Ann clearly encourages people to ask for what feels good for themselves- to **find a personal source of comfort**. For Ann, talking about her son and having others say his name- Ryan- brings him into conversation and gives Ann comfort. Even if it brings tears, hearing the name of your deceased loved one usually brings comfort. This is personal, so if you are supporting a grieving person, ask them what they want. Shall you share memories and stories? Shall you use his or her name? **Ask.** If you are a grieving person, this is a specific question for you to consider so that you can tell others around you your preference. **Advocate** for your own comfort needs.

Ann talks about Ryan in ways that paint a full, bright picture of him. And she manages to do something that helps her: she sees Ryan, and she sees someone else whom she calls "Heroin Ryan." She separates these two Ryans in her memory. During Ryan's fight with addiction, this separation allowed Ann and her husband to use a technique often suggested for families dealing with addiction: tough love. They could be tough when Ryan's behavior required this from them. They could welcome Ryan back home when he was not using.

Since Ryan's death, this **separation of memories** allows Ann to see the Ryan that was charming, caring and easy to love, separate from the addicted Ryan. It allows her to see the illness separate from her happy memories of her child. "It was not my choice," something Ryan said, is embedded in this bifurcated remembering. The matter of choice and substance use is a sensitive, personal zone for people grieving an addiction loss. **Finding ways to remember without overwhelming pain** is part of grief work.

When grief comes after the difficulty and turmoil of living with addiction, there are many complicating factors. Chronic stress and trauma take a toll on the body. People living with someone addicted to a chemical are always on, always waiting for the next bad thing to happen, always listening for the phone to ring. Their bodies stay geared up on the danger chemicals that are supposed to be for occasional crisis response. Blood pressure can be high, chemicals like adrenalin, cortisol, and epinephrine can be at unhealthy levels. People can be hypervigilant; Ann described this as being on "high alert."

Living with an addicted person means riding a roller coaster from hope to devastation and then back again, on an unpredictable track. For someone fighting the addiction of a loved one, it is as if they live with a tiger stalking them constantly, and all of the bodily danger signals that situation would bring. Our bodies cannot tell emotional stress from physical stress. The chemical response of the parasympathetic and sympathetic nervous system (our human emergency response system) is the same whether danger is real or anticipated. And, over time, that chemical response to stress can become chronic, so that a person's body never relaxes.

People grieving in the face of addiction both before and after a death need to **seek to change these automatic danger responses**. Ann explains how her use of breathing exercises and meditation have helped her to come off of "high alert," sleep better, and even lower her blood pressure. See the appendix of this book for some resources and specific exercises for managing chronic trauma.

CHAPTER FOUR

My Heart Will Always Be Broken

By Ellen Krohne

This is Alaina's story, as told by her mother, Elaine.

Elaine wrings her hands as we sit down. I can sense her dread to have this conversation one more time. Elaine and her experience were pivotal in establishing the Addiction Loss Support Group at Heartlinks Grief Center. She wanted to help others who were experiencing the same pain she'd been through. To help promote the new group, she and her husband told the story of their daughter Alaina's death to the local newspaper, so that people would understand why the support group was needed. So she's shared her story before.

I also notice her warm eyes and the smile lines that crease her face. She has an easy smile. She has a tattoo on her left wrist and I see her gently stroking it – subconsciously, I think. It says "Alaina." She notices me watching this and says, "It's the only one I have."

Elaine remembers her daughter's laugh. More specifically, her snort. She tells me how they both made a snorting sound when they laughed really hard, and that would make them laugh even more. She smiles broadly as she recalls this about her precious daughter, her and her husband Eric's only child.

Alaina means "dear child, one who is precious."

Elaine told me about her daughter and her addiction, in her words.

———//———

"She was a little girl who loved to play princess with her shiny tiara. She loved animals of all kinds. She liked to help people. She loved working with the developmentally disabled and older people. Alaina earned her Certified Nursing Assistant degree and worked at a local nursing home, too, before the demon got her. She was a good friend, and in high school she had a close circle of friends. She had a terrific sense of humor. She was not a good judge of character, though, especially in the boyfriend department. She had this radar that attracted assholes, it seemed.

Alaina adored my mother. It was mutual. She was the first granddaughter, and my mom loved her. I sometimes felt like I was just the vehicle in between that brought them together. Alaina was a year out of high school when her grandmother died of

Alzheimer's disease. Alaina stayed by her grandmother's side when she was in hospice. She didn't deal well with her death. Alaina kept things bottled up inside, like her dad, Eric, does.

Alaina wasn't what I'd describe as a happy child. I took her to a counselor in seventh grade to see what help they could give her. One other time later in high school, too. I believe she had an underlying depression that was never properly treated. Once she found them, the drugs helped make it bearable, somehow.

Alaina was an avid and gifted artist in school. After she died, I found a journal in her room from fifth grade. She wrote, "I feel like a ghost" and wondered, "What will my funeral be like?"

I often felt like Alaina was a lost soul – she didn't have enough hope. But I also didn't know what to do about it. We always just wanted her to be happy.

I knew she drank some and smoked pot in high school. I think they all did. She graduated from high school in 2006. It wasn't until she lost her job at a local coffee shop and started working at a nearby facility for the developmentally disabled that she started with the pills, I believe. She loved those kids and that job where she could feel like she was helping them. She was befriended by a co-worker who took "happy pills," as Alaina called them, for her anxiety, and shared those pills with her. That was the start.

She also hooked up with a guy – she was so "in love." We knew he wasn't right for her. We were worried because his brother was a heroin addict who had been arrested many times. But she moved in with this guy anyway, despite - or maybe because of - our objections. He was sharing the pills he was getting legally from some local doctor: OxyContin, Vicodin.

I was worried when Alaina got her tax refund in 2008 for $1,300.00, and it was all gone in a few months. With nothing to show how she spent it. She wouldn't admit where it went, either.

We played a game which I've since learned is one that lots of families of addicts play, called "You don't know and I don't use." An unspoken denial.

Pretty soon Alaina was snorting and smoking heroin with this boyfriend. It was much cheaper than the prescription drugs they could buy on the street. I could tell when she used by her cough the next morning. She had asthma and smoked cigarettes, too, but the heroin brought a specific type of ragged cough I'll never forget.

When I refused to pay half of the rent for her at this boyfriend's apartment, he kicked her out. She came back to our home. After she was using regularly, she drifted from job to job – at a gas station, a tanning salon, fast food restaurants. When she was working, she seemed better. But not the same. This demon had her. The drugs took over Alaina's soul, and she was a different person than before. Her temper would flare up in a second. She always seemed to be in a foul mood. She didn't want to be involved in family gatherings, which before she had enjoyed. Alaina was now like a stranger who was renting a room in our home.

She did what she had to do to get the drugs. And, I did what I had to do to keep her alive.

When Alaina left our home for work, I'd check her room to see what was missing. First her laptop, then her jewelry. Her precious pearls that she loved and had saved for. The tennis bracelet we'd bought her for Christmas. Even the Coach purses she loved. I'd notice checks missing from my checkbook. Not large sums, $20 or so, but constant. I didn't realize at the time, but do now, that heroin is cheap. You can get a "bud" for ten dollars – enough to get you high and stop the pain.

I slept with my keys and wallet under my pillow for years.

Eric and I went for a while to Nar-Anon, a support group for family members of addicts. At first it helped, but then as those around us reported how well their family members were doing, how rehab had helped and they were clean, it just depressed us. Alaina wasn't getting better. We quit going.

We couldn't do the "tough love" that so many recommended. Kick them out and don't relent. It wasn't right for us. I'd have never slept not knowing where she was, if she was dead on the street somewhere. I drove her sometimes to get her drugs so she wouldn't get sick. A mother can only watch her child get so ill before she will do almost anything to help ease the pain.

I'd give her $20.00 to buy gas or cigarettes, knowing she was actually getting her drugs, but also knowing she wouldn't be giving some guy a blow job for them.

Once Alaina went missing. We didn't know where she was and couldn't find her in any of the regular spots. The boyfriend forwarded an email to us that Alaina had sent him earlier that night. It read, "I've taken so much shit and still I can't die." We were terrified that this was it, that she had overdosed and we'd never find her. That this was the way it would end. We decided to call the sheriff and they found her later that night at a little roadside motel outside of our town. She answered the door and said, "I'm fine."

The end was not that night. A few more torturous years were ahead.

Alaina tried rehab. But my girl was not strong. She didn't make it the first time. We got her into a rehab facility in Quincy, Illinois, which was north of our town by a few hours, in 2012. On the third day Alaina called me and said, "Mom, come and get me or I will kill myself."

We didn't flinch. "No, you have to stay, you can't come home." She called the boyfriend and he went and got her. Of course, he denied he did. Said he'd not seen her when we asked. But the facility described him to a T, and his car, too. Addicts lie.

There is a difference between alcoholics and drug addicts. If an alcoholic is caught stealing your purse, they get angry for being accused. A drug addict who has stolen your purse will help you look for it. The addiction changes them.

Alaina broke it off with the boyfriend and came back home, eventually. Eric was walking the dog one night and saw her shooting up through the bedroom window. He'd quit smoking cold turkey, just decided he would one day. He just could not understand why she couldn't do the same with drugs. Eric saw things like that, just black or white – you use, then you stop. I can see gray a little better, so I played that role of champion for Alaina between us.

In May of 2013 Eric was diagnosed with esophageal cancer. I remember thinking, "God, how much more can you give me – how much do you expect me to take?" Alaina was shocked that her Dad was sick – he was always the strong one. He had chemo, then radiation before the surgery. A week after Eric came home from his surgery, I was unexpectedly hospitalized for a week. Alaina was home and was a good caregiver for him while I was ill. I was proud of her for that.

But I was terribly disappointed to discover that she stole six hundred dollars while I was gone. Like I said, the demon had her now. She had to have the drugs.

I told her once, when I was so frustrated with her lying and stealing, "It's your fault Dad got cancer – you stressed him too much with your addiction." I'll always regret telling her that, although I think it may be true.

In June of 2014, Alaina agreed to try rehab again. Well, maybe not agreed. It was a part of her sentence from an arrest earlier that year.

She overdosed at our house twice. The first time was a month after Eric's surgery, on Halloween night, 2013. Our little dog, Teddy, was barking like crazy at Alaina's bedroom door. I went in and she was face down on the bed. Her lips were blue. I remember thinking, "This is what she'll look like when she's dead."

Then thinking, "OK, I need to act, to get her back." I rolled her over and she started breathing again, and she was ok in a few minutes.

The next time was in February, 2014. I heard her fall. When I went into her room, she was breathing crazy and I couldn't wake her up. In a panic, I called 9-1-1. The paramedics came and the sheriff, too. By the time they got there, she was better and refused to go to the hospital. The sheriff arrested her for possession. The evidence was right there – the needle and spoon and traces of the heroin she'd injected. She went to jail for a few days. We posted her bond and went through the court process. She got community service and had to enter a program.

She went to rehab the second time as part of that program, following the arrest. In June 2014 she first went to a local hospital for detox, Touchette Regional Medical Center. The people there were incredible and so kind to her. From there she was to immediately enter Gateway Rehab, but was turned away since she was off of Eric's insurance now that she was 26. I was horrified and panicked. She'd just detoxed, she had to go somewhere.

I had worked for many years at the county Mental Health Board and my boss, one of the few people who knew of Alaina's addiction, found another center for her in Decatur, Illinois. I thank God for him. He did everything in his power to help us.

Alaina did really well there. She struggled, but was finally clean when she was discharged a month later.

At the center she met another guy. He was a military veteran and also a recovering addict from Central Illinois. They both wanted to stay clean, they swore, and they were, for about 90 days. Then we got the awful call that this boyfriend had relapsed and was in the hospital. Alaina went up to see him.

I knew in my heart at that moment that she would use again. After this boyfriend did, I just knew. Knew she would slip, too. This boyfriend was so sanctimonious, so full of preaching about what others should and shouldn't do. Eric and I felt a cold dread that Alaina was so smitten with him.

But it was the one time in Alaina's life that I would say she was truly happy. She loved him in a very different way, like you do someone who is meant for you. We wanted her to be happy, to believe her life was ahead of her. The last night I saw my daughter, she told me they were planning to get engaged in February.

They went back and forth between his house and ours, living, not working, and trying to stay clean, we prayed.

We had the family over for Thanksgiving that year, my dad and brothers and sisters. The house was full and the sounds of family were reassuring. Alaina and her new love left before dinner. They were gone quite a while, and the next day I realized that $200.00 was taken from my debit card. When Eric found out about the missing money, he was so hurt and mad that he kicked them both out of the house.

When she stole that money, I admitted it to myself for the first time. I knew it in my heart, knew that she wasn't going to make it. That she wasn't strong enough to beat the drugs. And even if she could, her body was shot. I didn't know then how soon it would be true.

Her health had been waning. Her feet and legs would swell and her cough was nonstop now. That fall, I had tried to get her to see a doctor, but she refused. "I'm fine, Mom," she said. I knew that they cut heroin with all kinds of stuff: baby laxatives, laundry detergent, starch, talcum power. Substances that don't dissolve and can lead to serious health problems as the particles build up or block arteries. In all those years of use she was slowly poisoning herself. My dad had commented at Thanksgiving, "Alaina looks bad – her eyes look dead."

We didn't see her again until her 27th birthday on December 1st. She came back home and we let her stay with us again. We wanted to believe she was clean, wanted to believe she hadn't been using.

One night a few days later, on December 9th, Alaina called out to me. I could hear the panic in her voice. She was in my bedroom and had her asthma nebulizer in her hand, all hunched over. She rasped, "Call an ambulance." I dialed 9-1-1 as fast as I could and they said to start CPR. When I ran back to the bedroom, I could tell she was dead. She'd fallen to the floor. There was fluid coming from her mouth and nose. They told me to keep doing CPR. I pulled her out into the hallway and did CPR. But my heart knew the truth. She was already gone.

Eric never came home early, but for some odd reason, this day he did. He walked in as the paramedics came, then the police. He was stunned and stood motionless at what he saw, his daughter lying lifeless in the hallway.

They took her out on a stretcher to the ambulance. The cops were combing through her room looking for evidence. This time, they found none.

The paramedics said I could not ride with her to the hospital. I drove myself while Eric stayed with the police. We were both in shock. What was happening? I let them talk me out of riding with her, and I will always regret that. I should have been there with her, holding her as she lost her battle.

The ambulance drove with the lights on but no siren. Not a good sign.

When I got to the hospital, they wouldn't let me see her. I was ushered into a room to wait. I wasn't crying. Just praying and thinking, "Is she dead, is it over?"

A chaplain came into the room. This must have been his first day on the job because he was just not helpful. First, he said, "Is she your only child?"

I said, "Yes."

Then he said, "Well, then, this is going to be bad for you."

I said, "Wouldn't matter, one or ten, if your child is dead, it's bad, don't you think?"

Thank God he left and a nurse that was at the desk came and sat kindly, just listening to me. I was telling her all about Alaina. The Alaina before the drugs. The Alaina I'll always love.

I called my girlfriend, and she came. Eric arrived soon after. The doctor came in and told us she was gone. He asked if we wanted to see her.

They had cleaned her up. Alaina lay on the bed. So peaceful. So beautiful. We kissed and hugged her and talked to her. Eric rubbed her head like he did when she was little. She had two pink tears on her face. I gently wiped those away.

The coroner came in and said they had to do toxicology tests, to find out what killed her. The conclusion was to be that she had died of a massive heart attack. We were, in a small way, relieved that she didn't die of an overdose. But she was dead from the drugs, just the same.

I felt it right to call her boyfriend to let him know. He said to me, a mother that just lost her child, "Alaina had told me what horrible parents you were." Gasping for air, I hung up.

By this time, it was nearly 11 p.m. We went home, exhausted. Our hearts were broken, but neither of us had cried at the hospital. Later I would reflect that this most horrific outcome had been in our mind for years. While it was sudden that day and shocking, we both knew it was coming.

We got home and realized that our dog, Jack, was not there. The police officers must have left him out. As we looked for him, I completely lost it. Then I got mad at myself for being so upset about the missing dog, when my daughter had just died. This was the first of many emotions that would be hard to understand in the years ahead.

We didn't sleep at all. At 3 a.m. the phone rang and it was the funeral home, asking, "What kind of service do you want for her?" Eric said, "What the hell, it's 3 a.m., we will call you later this morning!" They gave some lame answer about the law saying they had to contact us within so many hours, but it was sure not appreciated.

We decided to have Alaina cremated, and not to have a memorial service. We didn't want to share her with anyone, especially those that had enabled her drug use, like her boyfriends. All her other friends had long ago dropped her.

We saw and drew comfort from postings on her Facebook page. From old friends that had written nice things about Alaina, like, "You helped me so much in my life." I wondered why some of them couldn't have done that for her, been there for her.

We've constructed a shrine for our girl. A beautiful cabinet in our house holds her urn and some of our favorite photos of her and her favorite things. The shiny little tiara she adored as a child now sits atop her urn."

Elaine described her life to me as she journeys through grief.

———//———

"The first year, I slept all the time. It was a numb blur. My friend suggested, "Let's pretend she's on a vacation and you just can't reach her." That worked for a little while. Not long.

The second year it began to sink in. I'm never going to trip over her shoes again. I couldn't sleep at all at night, and then would fall asleep in the afternoon, exhausted. I was like a baby, with my nights and days mixed up.

The third year was not great, either, but little bits and pieces of acceptance started to surface and there were some days when I almost felt ok.

Part of the problem, I think, was that I retired right at the same time that Alaina died. So, I had two big life-changing events happen at once. I hadn't prepared for either change.

I'm an avid reader, and it just makes me crazy that all those grief books talk about the "stages of grief." Like it's a linear process and you move neatly from one phase to the next to, "Oh, I'm feeling fine. All better. All done."

That's crap. It's not like that AT ALL!! I'd think I was doing pretty good, maybe moving forward, and I'd be right back to the beginning. Not even able to function. Not able to get out of bed.

Each day was like a new Day One. Each day was a process. This day – maybe I can get out of bed. Maybe I can laugh. Or cry. Or maybe neither, just be numb. Each day was like a new Day One.

I remember the first time I went to Walmart. I felt invisible. Here I saw myself all bloody, all beaten, and no one saw me. No one acknowledged me. I was just invisible.

Grief blew my life apart. Things kept going on around me, but I was blown apart. My teeny part of the world, my speck in the universe, and I felt imploded even in that teeny part. All cracked up and broken.

I think people in general look at a drug addict's death differently than death by other illnesses. Maybe like they do suicide. "Your child made a choice to be addicted." I knew in my heart that's what lots of people thought. They thought, "She got what she deserved, she was an addict, she was a piece of shit."

One of my own family at a christening the next year, was going on and on about "Put all those drug dealers and addicts in jail." Then she looked right at me and caught herself and backtracked her words, before she said anything even more hateful.

My young niece said to me, "Your grief is different than if Alaina had died of cancer, because she made a choice."

Some people just feel bad for you, and don't know what to say. One thing I absolutely hate is when someone says, "I know how you feel." Followed by, "My brother died last year." Or some other family member. Even if it was a child, they don't know my pain, what we went through with her addiction, and it maddens me that they think they do.

The other thing it changed is how I look at life, and valuing each day with those I love. I treasure very much my nephew. He calls every week, just to see how we're doing. He calls me on Alaina's birthday and on her death anniversary. He understands just his caring, just that phone call, is what I need.

Looking back, I should have tried harder to be kind to myself after she died. To not do what you don't want to or can't yet do, but that others ask or expect you to.

For example, Alaina died on December 9th and that year my brother, who always hosted Christmas, decided to go to Colorado for Christmas. That left my Dad and other brother, whose wife had died, with no place to go. So instead of another relative stepping up, knowing it would be too much for us, they let us host Christmas. It didn't go well. Eric had a very hard time throughout the day. My Dad asked, "What's wrong?"

I told him, "Eric's in pain."

Dad thought for a moment and then asked, "From his surgery?"

"No, Dad, he's in pain from the fact that Alaina just died."

A few hours later my sister-in-law kept insisting that Eric find this movie she wanted to watch on TV. We'd just gotten a new system and he couldn't figure it out. Eric finally got mad and stomped out. I wanted to scream at them, "What assholes you are.

If you weren't all so self-absorbed you wouldn't have let us have this dinner – we aren't able yet." Not a merry Christmas memory. The point is, each person should try hard to understand their own limits, and don't let others push you before you are ready.

Eric coped with his grief by working. He is a train engineer, and he had all these pictures on his phone of Alaina. He looked at them as he worked, and changed them as he chugged along. He had a hard time, I know, but dealt with it more within himself. I know it upsets him, and it hits him hard still when other people complain about their children.

We talk about Alaina a lot. We keep her in our thoughts every day. I feel so fortunate that losing Alaina has brought Eric and I even closer together. We share that we were the two who loved her the most.

But while Eric had his work and his stoic way of getting through his grief, I struggled. I was the one home every day. The one home doing all the cleaning up, getting rid of her stuff. One day I'm a mom, and the next day I'm not. I had a lot of love in me with no place to share it.

I thank God on a daily basis for Randy's Rescue Ranch near our home. I started volunteering there in October 2017. I have always had a passion for animals, like Alaina did. I went to volunteer and the first day they gave me a shovel and said, "Go clean up the horse shit from the stables." Another volunteer showed me what to do. And you know what, I just fell in love with the place. There is an old donkey there, I just fell in love with her. There are lots of dogs, some in hospice. I can give the animals lots of love. Everyone that volunteers there is wounded in some way, and we all talk about it. It saved me.

My advice for everyone grieving is, when you are able, find something that is your passion, like the animals are mine, and GO FOR IT!

I also feel blessed that God has always been with me through this journey. Blessed that God knew Alaina was struggling and took her before something really bad happened. God let me be right there with her as she died, He didn't let her die alone or with someone else.

I can see now, four years later, how important it is to be able to put all the bullshit you went through aside, put how they acted once they were in drug's grip aside. That was not your child. That was the demon, the monster that took them over. Remember and cherish how they were before.

It's hard, but try to be good to yourself. Don't be embarrassed. Your child made a fatal mistake that wasn't your choice.

I learned from losing Alaina that my heart, it will always be broken. I will grieve for her until I die. Not as intensely as the first few years, but the grief, it is always there, a part of me. Her absence is like a physical presence, like an empty chair next to me.

If I could change anything it would be the way we deal with rehab for addicts. This needs to be completely overhauled. They need to be able to go whether they are insured or not. The system releases them in 21-28 days, which is way too short. They let them out at the most vulnerable time. They don't treat the real issues, like depression or other mental illness. I don't think we will ever win the war on drugs. It's just too big a business.

In a word, I'd describe the last decade as "horrible." Her addiction, her death, the years of grief that followed. The wonderful thing we cling to is our memory of her before. And the knowledge that Eric and I have already lived through the worst thing we could ever imagine, so no matter what happens, we're good now."

Alaina at age 25

My Heart Will Always Be Broken
– Grief Reflections –
By Diana Cuddeback, LCSW

Aliana's life and her loss created a mosaic of long-term struggle, attempts to handle mental health issues, and emotional pain. Her death propelled her mother to create the Addiction Loss Support Group. This story teaches important grief lessons that start with Elaine's strong suggestion that a grieving person needs to **prioritize themselves**. Family tradition, others' needs, the way people are used to doing holidays – all need to take a backseat to the grieving person "understanding their own limits." Elaine teaches us that when you are grieving you need to tune into your own needs and not feel pressured by outside people and circumstances. This is part of the grief experience that is so dislocating. You may have had the Thanksgiving Dinner at your house for years, but now you have no heart for it. **Respect yourself and your limits.**

This vital teaching brings up something else you should know about: Ring Theory. Not the algebra Ring Theory, but the **Comfort-In-Dump-Out Ring Theory** put forth by Susan Silk and Barry Goldman in a 2013 Los Angeles Times article. It is a model suggesting a compassionate way of managing interactions with people who were impacted by a difficult or traumatic life experience. It works like this:

Draw a series of concentric rings around the person who has had the horrible life event. That person is in the center. Move out from there, placing people less directly impacted by the event in circles, expressing their distance from event impact. The person in the center ring (most directly impacted by the difficult event) can say anything he/she wants to anyone, anywhere, anytime. He or she can talk and protest and whine and wail and swear at the universe. This person can shout and say, "Life is unfair" and "Why me?" That's the one and only compensation for being in the center ring.

Everyone else can say those things too, but only to people in larger rings. When you are talking to a person in a ring smaller than yours, someone closer to the center of the crisis, the goal is to provide comfort and support. ***Comfort in.***

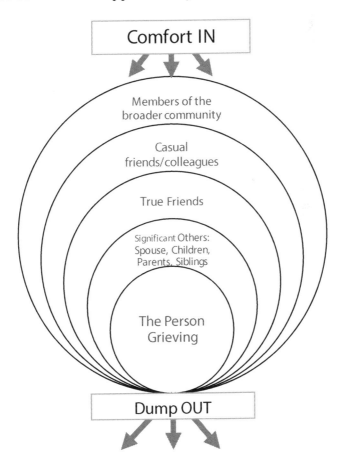

If you want to scream or cry or complain, if you want to tell someone how stunned you are or how shaken up you feel, or if you want to drone on about how it reminds you of all the horrible things that have happened to you, that's fine. It's a normal response. Just do it to someone in a bigger ring. Don't do it with a person in a smaller ring. ***Dump Out.***

Using Ring Theory to insulate yourself as a grieving person from unnecessary pain and aggravation, to provide self-compassion, and to help yourself set limits, is an important tool. It will help you prioritize where to spend your physical and emotional energy. If someone in an outer ring is frustrating you, like the person in Elaine's story who was fussing about watching a movie on TV, it is easier to dismiss the negativity remembering the directive **Comfort IN, Dump OUT.** If you are seeking to support a grieving person, use Ring Theory to help guide your interactions. When in doubt, be quiet and be present. Comfort in.

Elaine also gives us another grief teaching: **Educate and Advocate**. If you are grieving, copy the Ring Theory article and share it, add it to your Facebook wall, post it on your fridge, create your own personal illustration and put specific names on it. Most people are just self-absorbed and inconsiderate, not really mean (though a few are mean, I know.) It is unfair that you, as a grieving person, must educate others. It is disappointing that people you thought would be helpful are not. It is rotten that you must advocate for your right to prioritize your needs. But you have to. Taking charge of these activities can really help you avoid feeling stuck and helpless.

Elaine has two more ideas that are key to managing grief. She explains that the need to **find a place to invest love and energy** is vital. She has found a ranch for abused animals where a combination of physical work and an opportunity to share her loving energy has given her comfort. Working there has allowed her to **find the passion** that lives inside of her and needs expression. That passion is there after all the years of struggle and after all the pain of loss. It has also helped her find a community of other people managing their wounds by doing something positive. Someone gave her a shovel on her first day and told her to "go shovel horse shit." Perhaps part of healing from your grief will be to find your own way to "shovel shit."

Finding community is Elaine's final big teaching for anyone living with loss. Elaine created the Addiction Loss Support Group at the Heartlinks Grief Center to create a place where people wounded by the fight of and loss to addiction can find community. Alaina's continuing presence in the world is manifest in this community which her mother created out of grief and loss. Group is both heartbreaking and heartwarming. People laugh and cry, share ugly secrets, and stand amazed at the things they have experienced. In this group, people know one another's children and lost loved ones, not as addicts but as whole people. There is a wry and patient understanding when new members join, as they are just starting to manage the early parts of their own grief. There is time and space, love and patience in that group. Sometimes there is overwhelming sadness. But in that group, there is community, and no one has to feel completely alone.

CHAPTER FIVE

His Higher Power
By Ellen Krohne

This is Johnny's story, as told by his father, Sam.

"I quit drinking for good nineteen years ago. I don't tell many people, because most people think that once you're a drinker you always will be one," Sam starts our discussion. Sam's loss has been very recent, just six months ago. He looks down at the floor, fidgeting in his chair as I start explaining the interview process and what's ahead. He looks up at me and I can see his soft eyes brimming with tears. I can sense he's not really ready to talk about his son's story, so we start with his.

Since this family's loss is so recent, he has asked to make this story anonymous.

———⁄⁄———

"God helps everybody."
—Johnny's father, Sam

"I quit because drinking ruined part of my life. I drank away my marriage and set a bad example for my kids. I had no friends. I am bipolar, have been diagnosed for decades.

It was a therapist I saw for my bipolar condition that asked me first, "Are you an alcoholic, Sam?" I wasn't sure. I'd drank five beers before our appointment (first time I did that before seeing her), which was kind of normal for me after work. But I didn't know if that qualified me as an alcoholic. She directed me to a local open meeting of Alcoholics Anonymous (AA) near our home in Collinsville.

Well, I couldn't find that meeting, so I went home with a twelve pack and finished that off. I did make it to the next AA meeting. It was pretty obvious I was one – an alcoholic. I went to a few meetings and figured out I needed a sponsor. The sponsor is like a guide, an encourager, for the newcomer to the AA Twelve Step Program. I learned that a sponsor can soon become your best friend.

I asked a few people, but didn't find that right sponsor to do the steps with me. I went that first time a couple of years without a drink. It didn't last. I never felt like I fit in with AA, so I fit myself out. I started drinking again, now only worse. Let's see, that was about 1998. Maureen, my ex-wife, had already divorced me and I moved back home, back to Chicago.

Maureen, she is pretty much the opposite of me. She is organized and productive. I am not. She has always had a lot of friends. I had none. She is a good Catholic girl from a large Catholic family that were drinkers, too.

Before I met her, I'd done some drugs, too. Cocaine, but not heroin. I was scared of heroin, that was for junkies. I stopped all that when I met her. When I asked her dad for her hand in marriage, I brought two cases of beer with me. He drank me right under the table. Before I passed out, he said, "Yes, you have my permission." I was respectful and called him Mister. He liked that, too, I think.

We got married in 1988 and made our home in the suburbs of Chicago. I had a good job, working for a laboratory there. We had Johnny in 1990. In 1992 our home got broken into and we were robbed. No one was hurt, but Maureen was scared to stay there. Her dad came and moved them out, back to Collinsville. I followed a few months later after I got the house fixed up and sold.

Johnny was this bright-eyed, adorable, red-haired little wonder. He was a very smart kid, clever I'd call it. Parents, other kids, everyone loved him, just were attracted to his smile and gentle ways. He got a lot of attention.

When Johnny was a kid, Maureen was his best influence, but I was his hero. You could tell. I was doing odd jobs for a living when we moved back to Collinsville, and Johnny would sit on the porch with Maureen waiting for me to come home. He'd shout, "Daddy, Daddy!" when I'd pull up, and he'd jump off the porch into my arms. I like to remember that now.

We had Ryan in 1993. Just the two boys. I sure wasn't settling down as a father though. Before we divorced, what my boys saw was me coming home and drinking until I passed out. After I quit AA our marriage was over, in reality it was already over before I quit. I moved back to Chicago in 1998. I could make more money there and had child support to pay. I did some drugs for a while, cocaine mostly, and drank lots, but soon couldn't afford the drugs. You can only do that if you have lots of money.

By the next year I'd had enough of that life and found an AA chapter in Chicago. I figured it out – you have to find a sponsor and really commit to going through the Twelve Steps, not just want to not drink, but to want to do the program. And, I'd found God. I was ready.

I started really praying, asking God to help me – to help me to clean house and be able to help others. I didn't think I deserved it, and wasn't sure He would, but I came to realize that God helps everybody. I kept praying for Him to help me. And He did. It took a year for me with my sponsor to work through the program, but I stuck with it. I've been sober since 1999.

Meanwhile, Johnny was getting into trouble. I found out he was using drugs when he was 15, in 2005. I was sick when I realized he'd done hard drugs, things I was scared of, like heroin.

I thought he was on the right path. He was athletic and tall, a star basketball player before this drug thing started. His intermural team went undefeated. He knew how to set up the ball and was just amazing to watch. I wanted him to be a basketball player. I like to remember that, too.

But his choice to do drugs changed that path. Maureen called and told me he was in a local treatment center. Johnny, I soon realized, would be a "box-checker" – someone who did everything right, to check the boxes to be released. Did what he needed to get the court off his back. And then relapse as soon as he could get his hands on his drug.

He was attracted to the group that wanted to use drugs, like he did. They were all using and in trouble. I don't think he was the leader, just followed along. He was in treatment four times during high school. He got two DUI's and totaled two cars. Luckily, he didn't kill anyone. He would get arrested and the court would order him to rehab. He'd go and get out and relapse right away. I wasn't there much, so Maureen dealt with all the day-to-day drama and trauma he caused.

Early in his drug journey, Johnny stole from me. I took pain killers and muscle relaxers, all different types of psych drugs. I was on a merry-go-round of different drugs until they found the right combination for my bipolar disorder. Johnny stole my medication just one time. I told him I would beat the crap out of him if he touched them again, and he never did. He just got those pills from other sources on the street. It wasn't long before he was trying all kinds of drugs and found the heroin. That and alcohol were his drugs of choice.

Even with all the absences from high school for rehab, he was able to get into Southern Illinois University at Carbondale. He was such a smart kid. He told us he was majoring in business. I knew he went there to party. And that he did. He flunked out in six months because he spent way more time getting high then going to class and studying. I never understood how he could afford the drugs. We didn't send him much money.

A couple of years later, it became clear how he'd funded his drug use. He was arrested and sent to federal prison for one year for counterfeiting. After prison he went to a halfway house, and soon was using drugs again. I think he was so into drugs and that culture that he didn't know another path to take, and rehab centers didn't work for him. He was on the "drug bus," as he called it, and couldn't get off.

I moved back to the Collinsville area when Maureen and her new husband called, saying they couldn't handle Johnny anymore. She told me, "One of them (meaning her husband or Johnny) was going to go to jail for murder. Johnny can't stay here anymore." She made me a deal. She knew I was struggling in Chicago, working as a salesperson. She offered to pay my rent, food and utilities, basically to support me while I got on my feet here, if I moved back and took Johnny in to live with me.

Wow! I figured this would be difficult. I knew I had to lay down the law with Johnny; he had to abide by my rules or he was out. I told him that I had worked too hard to get sober and treasured my sobriety – you are not screwing that up.

Well, it worked for a while. I found a job as a night janitor. One night late I got a call from Johnny. He'd had an accident and been arrested for DUI. He didn't take the test, didn't blow. It cost him his driver's license, a fine, and my respect. He lied to me when I asked him if he was drinking. I could tell he had been. I guess he forgot my past experience with alcohol.

But I bailed him out and gave him one more chance. If you screw up again, you are on the street and I'll go back to Chicago, I told him.

I realize looking back, I was in denial. He was using drugs, but I didn't want to admit it. I didn't want to kick him out like that, where he'd be on the street and die in an alley, where the rats would get him.

He had a young girlfriend, around 19, a real beauty. He was such a good-looking guy he always had a girlfriend. She was a heroin addict, too. I told him he had to get a job and he did. They both worked as temps at a part-time staffing agency, and made enough to get drugs. I kept praying the same prayer I did when I went to AA the second time, "Lord, please help him."

I begged him to come to AA with me. I knew if I could get him to try, it might work for him. It did for me, and I think we are, or were, a lot alike.

He went one more time to rehab. He went, court-ordered, to a detox treatment center in Central Illinois. When he was getting kicked out because they found out that insurance wouldn't cover his treatment, he had no one else to call, so he called me. I went and got him. I prayed all the way up there for God to help him.

As we drove home, silently, Johnny softly said, "Dad, you have been sober for eighteen years. I'm going to try it your way." The words I'd prayed so hard to hear.

I asked my AA sponsor, Edward, to be his sponsor. Edward had been in AA for 37 years sober and was very respected in AA circles. Edward said, "I am impressed with him – more than any other person I've sponsored." Edward was thorough. He made newcomers work through the Twelve Steps in fine detail, ensuring they were committed, especially Step Four and Step Five. These are:

"Step Four. Made a searching and fearless moral inventory of ourselves.

Step Five. Admitted to God, to ourselves, and to another human being the exact nature of our wrongs."

And Johnny did. He started AA right after I got him back from the detox treatment center. In early 2018, he was clean and sober. Just as I prayed, God helped him. He helps everyone. The members of my AA club, my friends I now cherish, they went from hating his drug-using guts for what he'd put me through, to enjoying his sense of humor. Everyone there liked him now that he was sober.

They wanted him to do well. I was proud of him.

Johnny had gotten a job through an AA member and was working now, as a tree trimmer. He seemed to enjoy the physical labor and it was helping him stay sober. I bought Johnny a truck to help him get to work. He was on the right path; I was sure of it.

It was time for him to get up for work on that Wednesday morning, May 2nd 2018. Around 7 a.m., Ryan had called and wanted to borrow the truck, so I was planning to drive Johnny to work. Ryan and Johnny hadn't been close – Ryan didn't like his drug use and made no bones about it. But they were seeing each other more in those last months. I think, no I know, Ryan was pulling for Johnny in those last two months.

Ryan found the front door open, which was odd. Ryan's screaming woke me, and my first thought was, "Are those boys going to have a fight?" Then, I didn't hear Johnny, just Ryan screaming at the top of his lungs, "No, No. He's not breathing, not talking."

I jumped out of bed and frantically put on my jeans and t-shirt. Johnny's face was a deep purple. He was face down in the pillow. His legs were covered in red splotches. I said, "Get some water, Ryan, throw some water on him to wake him up." That had worked once the year before when he'd overdosed. It brought him back to breathing. I was just stunned at how he looked. Thinking to myself, "What happened?" But knowing in my heart what had happened.

The water didn't revive him. He was cold to the touch. We called 911. Four or five police came. They didn't use the Narcan or even try to bring him back. They said he'd been dead for hours. The police called an ambulance and the attendant took some blood from my dead son. Said they would take him to the nearest funeral home, unless we had another choice. I don't even remember answering them. I was just numb, just couldn't believe what I saw, what had happened. But I knew I had to be strong for Ryan.

I got my wits about me and called Maureen. Her husband was in the hospital ready to have knee surgery, but she came right over. So distraught, this strong woman was just distraught.

I called my AA sponsor, Edward, and he had me come right to the AA club building. He said, "We'll lock up, and you do what you have to do." We talked about Why? Why God would let this happen. Why did Johnny use that day, when he was doing so well? I'll never understand.

Even though we had been to church two Sundays in a row before Johnny died, I believe the answer is that Johnny hadn't found his Higher Power. In AA, finding your Higher Power, a power greater than ourselves, whatever that may be, is imperative to progress. I think Johnny's Higher Power was maybe his girlfriend, maybe the heroin itself yet. He just hadn't had time to find it. How I wish he could have.

The bloodwork showed he died from a drug overdose. Heroin and Fentanyl. A lethal dose of Fentanyl.

We had a visitation for Johnny on the 5th of May. All of the family were there. The AA friends he'd made so recently all came. A lot of my friends came – we try to be with our own, our AA own, in tough situations. Lots of his high school classmates, old girlfriends. One high school friend had driven three hours on a motorcycle to get there. Most of them didn't know for sure he was a heroin addict. Only close family and the people at AA knew."

Below is Johnny's obituary, written by his mom. It expresses well how this gentle boy struggled.

Johnny, 28, died, Wednesday, May 2, 2018. When you look at Johnny's picture, I'm sure you see a handsome young man, full of youthful innocence with a bright future – the typical "boy next door." He was all that, plus an incredibly smart, caring, witty individual with an amazing sense of humor. To know him was to love him, and he had an extremely unique outlook on life.

What you don't see is the pain and struggle he lived with for years, and the demons he battled every day. He loved life, was looking forward to many tomorrows, and was making plans for the future. But in the end, the demons won, and a beautiful life was cut short…just like so many others we all hear about in today's news.

So, please – love fully, smile, and be kind to others. Don't judge too harshly or too quickly, as you never know what issues people are facing or what struggles they may be dealing with…a kind word or gesture and a smile can go a very long way.

————//————

Sam continued. Still fidgeting in his chair a little, but now smiling at me. My heart hurts for him as I assure Sam that he is doing very well telling me his son's story. Sam struggles to put in words the path his grief journey is taking.

————//————

"No words can describe how I feel.

I'm not much fun to be around since Johnny died. I keep trying to express how I feel and I just can't. Most people don't want me to talk about him. The only people that let me talk about it now, just six months later, are my home group at AA. They let me talk. Others think I should just get over it. Heartlinks Grief Support Group is the other place I feel safe, I can talk there.

I miss Johnny. I miss how he'd let me tease him, just in fun, and he'd laugh. Living with him was rough, for sure, but he gave me purpose. Now, I just don't have a map. I just eat to live; I've lost almost 20 pounds. I'm still going through it.

I'm doing more with God now. I've started daily readings and devotionals. Real focused prayer. That helps me cope with this pain. I think I was kind of a slacker before, but now, I'm praying and working hard to be a good person, a good sponsor.

I pray for Johnny. I don't know where Johnny is – he didn't get born again that I know. But he was baptized as a Catholic and his Mom saw to it that he grew up with faith. So, I have to trust he'll be there when I get there, to heaven.

I think to stem this crisis, to stop losing kids to drugs, we need to learn more. Learn more from those in jails and on the street. From the criminals themselves, the drug users and dealers. Ask them why they use, how they lure kids in, how they sell and where they get their drugs. And then teach our kids to be wise about drugs.

When kids get addicted, they need professional help. They don't need to be around those friends that will lead them right back to drugs. I think if more programs used the AA Twelve Steps, and other programs like it, that may help people to stay clean. But in the end, the person has to want to and be ready to be sober. It can't be forced. Alcohol and drugs are cunning, baffling and powerful, so it's best that you don't do it alone. There is strength in numbers. The important things are to find God, clean house, and help others.

I'm never going to stop missing Johnny. I don't have the words to describe it, but I just know my boy was too gentle to run with the wolves."

> *"The main thing is that he be willing
> to believe in a Power greater than himself
> and that he lives by spiritual principles."*
> —Alcoholics Anonymous

Alcoholic Anonymous: The Twelve Steps

Step 1: We admitted we were powerless over alcohol—that our lives had become unmanageable.

Step 2: Came to believe that a Power greater than ourselves could restore us to sanity.

Step 3: Made a decision to turn our will and our lives over to the care of God *as we understood Him.*

Step 4: Made a searching and fearless moral inventory of ourselves.

Step 5: Admitted to God, to ourselves, and to another human being the exact nature of our wrongs.

Step 6: Were entirely ready to have God remove all these defects of character.

Step 7: Humbly asked Him to remove our shortcomings.

Step 8: Made a list of all persons we had harmed, and became willing to make amends to them all.

Step 9: Made direct amends to such people wherever possible, except when to do so would injure them or others.

Step 10: Continued to take personal inventory, and when we were wrong promptly admitted it.

Step 11: Sought through prayer and meditation to improve our conscious contact with God, *as we understood Him*, praying only for knowledge of His will for us and the power to carry that out.

Step 12: Having had a spiritual awakening as the result of these Steps, we tried to carry this message to alcoholics, and to practice these principles in all our affairs.

Even though this story is anonymous, the family asked for a photo of their son to be included.

His Higher Power
– Grief Reflections –
Diana Cuddeback, LCSW

This story is one of generational addiction. A father grieving a son, a burst of hope, and a short promise of connection. A son lost after a struggle. Possibilities lost, but continuing connections and a sense of community remaining as a support through grief. Sam speaks of using the support he found through a recovery community and Twelve Step program before, during, and after Johnny's fight with addiction.

Sam offers us many clear and down-to-earth ideas for managing grief. His paradigm comes from years of immersion in Twelve Step support programs. **Focusing on spirituality**, "finding my higher power," continues to be an ongoing support for Sam. He used his spirituality to navigate his own addiction, his son's addiction, and he continues to plug into this resource since Johnny's death. **Prayer, daily readings and devotions** are helpful to navigate the grief process. Sam explains how intensely he is using these techniques to traverse the lost and lonely places of his grief. He explains that he has no words for his loss, yet he explores and reads the thoughts of others to seek solace and understanding. Sam describes his openness to support as well.

While Sam struggles to express his loss, he has found safe spaces where he is free to articulate and explore his feelings with others who understand or care. **Seeking support** is important in managing grief. There are many support options. It takes effort and investment to really develop and use support groups. It means you must be open to the experiences, thoughts, feelings, and opinions of others as you seek to create a community of people that will share one another's pain.

If you try a support group, expect it to feel uncomfortable, even awkward, but also expect it to get better after a few sessions. Be willing to invest in three sessions. If you absolutely don't feel a fit, or if it just feels wrong for you, move on. If you are grieving a loss with a partner, understand that using group support may be something you cannot do together. It might be useful for you both, but sometimes it is not right for both people in a relationship, or for all people in a family. Remember, grief is an individual experience even when you share the same loss.

The powerful support Sam has received from his AA sponsor has been vital. Not everyone needs a sponsor to navigate their grief, but the idea of one or two key people who are willing to be present, as Sam explains that his sponsor was for him right after Johnny's death, to "lock up and do what we have to do"- that kind of support is powerful. Alan Wolfelt, a psychologist who has made a career focusing on grief, talks about the act of **companioning** the grieving. To "companion" is to be fully present to someone else's pain, not to guide or teach, but to watch and learn from them. A companion bears witness to another's pain without trying to take it away. If you are grieving, finding a companion who can care in this way may be helpful. If you care for someone struggling with grief, consider whether this is something you can provide. Not all of us are created with the ability to be a companion, however. There is a beautiful quote by the theologian Henri Nouwen that captures the essence of companioning:

"When we honestly ask ourselves which person in our lives means the most to us, we often find that it is those who, instead of giving advice, solutions, or cures, have chosen rather to share our pain and touch our wounds with a warm and tender hand. The friend who can be silent with us in a moment of despair or confusion, who can stay with us in an hour of grief and bereavement, who can tolerate not knowing, not curing, not healing, and face with us the reality of our powerlessness, that is a friend who cares."

—Henri Nouwen, Out of Solitude:
Three Meditations on the Christian Life

CHAPTER SIX

I Laugh to Keep from Crying
By Ellen Krohne

This is Melody's story, as told by her mother, Ann.

> *"The human race has one really effective weapon, and that is laughter."*
> —Mark Twain

Ann was my fourth interview. I'd already heard heart-wrenching stories of losing a child to drugs, and then losing them forever. I didn't think it could get worse. But Ann's story felt like not just the loss of a child, but of a family torn apart, with losing a child the final outcome. Some of what happened to them is almost unthinkable, but it did happen. Some of it made me laugh.

Because there is still an ongoing investigation, all of the names have been changed in this story.

The word I'd use to describe Ann when I met her is jovial. A ready smile, cracking jokes at herself and making me laugh. When she started crying, though, the flood gates opened and I saw how much pain that outward jovial nature attempted to hide.

———— // ————

"My husband and I had been married for 36 years in 2015. We had two girls. Lenn was born in March 1982. Melody was a New Year's Baby in 1986. John and I had our struggles, but we were reasonably happy, I thought.

John and I would argue, and when I mentioned divorce, he'd cry, "Don't leave me." I found out later he told others that he just didn't want to leave me with the kids.

We had gone to counseling early in our marriage, in our early 20's. Well, that sure wasn't a good idea – HA! John developed a crush on our counselor. He'd bring her up periodically. When the counselor was hospitalized and John found out, he went and visited her. She was married and dedicated to her husband, though. Years later, when the counselor's husband died, John changed. He was different – he lost 100 pounds, bought a Mustang, was ready to impress her, I guess. But they never got together. John called it his own "Greek Tragedy." Whatever.

I'd been seeing a counselor and was just not doing any better in my struggle with John's verbal abuse. I had been hospitalized and was on medication that was working for me, but John and I were not making progress, and I felt unsafe in our home. When I shared that with my counselor, she called the Violence Prevention Center and I went there for a month.

John and I went to a couple of counseling sessions after that month, and we didn't make progress then either. He asked me for a divorce in late 2015.

I was hurt, after all these years. John was verbally abusive all through our marriage, but he was a good person, I thought. He'd say things he knew would hurt me, just to get a reaction from me. He would call me crazy all the time. I never did understand why. He told our daughter, Lenn, that he wanted me to come home instead of divorcing, and he'd drive me crazy. Maybe he found out how much a divorce cost.

I was so down, felt so worthless, I tried to commit suicide by taking a bunch of pills. I called my brother who I'd always been close to, to say goodbye. He called an ambulance and they took me to the hospital.

I went to live with my daughter, Lenn, after that. She had a small home and a husband and kids. I didn't even have a bed. I knew I couldn't stay there long. A divorce cost way more money than I had, and John hadn't filed either. We were in limbo for almost a year.

My brother, whom I also worked for and was so close to, gave me the money to file for divorce. John was pissed – he had to give me half of his retirement, half of everything. I don't think he'd thought about that. But, heck, he was the one that asked for it. Even though he makes out now like I was the one that asked, since I filed. Whatever. I had a right to my share.

Our Melody, she stayed with John when I left. She was 28 and had two little boys. Steve was born in 2006. His father isn't in the picture, never really was. Corey was born in 2010 and his father has always been in his life, but Melody had custody of them both.

Melody worked as a bartender. She was full of life and a beautiful girl. Beautiful like a movie star – not just because she

91

was mine, but she really was. Lots of people said she should be in movies – she just didn't have the money or the confidence to go there.

When she was a little girl, she was that happy, darling child. She loved the sky – the moon and the stars, they were her favorite things from little on. She loved to make movies with our video camera, to make us laugh. Once she made a movie called, "Dog Making a Poop." It was hilarious. Once she forgot to turn off the camera and made one of herself making a poop. HA!

She was also one tough cookie. She could take care of herself, stand up for herself. And she'd defend herself. Once a guy in the bar called her a vulgar name and she jumped over the bar and threw him out.

Trouble like that seemed to follow her. Not her fault, it just followed her. One time, while I was in the shelter, she was getting gas and two men harassed her. I'm not sure why. Her son, Corey, was in the car and she didn't want him to hear what they were saying, so she knocked that guy flat out.

Yet, she was tender, she'd be upset if someone was hurt or hurting. Especially if she'd inflicted it. HA!

When she was a teenager, she told her Dad she'd tried cocaine and needed help. She liked it, and was worried she would get addicted. John wasn't very active in their lives, that was left to me. But Melody knew what my reaction would be. And when I found out, I came unglued and cried and cried. Just like she knew I would. But I got her to a counselor.

I went with her to this counselor and we were arguing, like we always did, back and forth. The counselor stood up and said,

"I can't be of service to you – I cannot help her." I figured he was taken aback at the way we talked to each other, I'm not sure. I broke down and cried and cried right there.

But, Melody promised, "I'll never do anything again, don't cry, Mom. I hate it when you cry, stop crying!"

And, I don't believe she did. Not as a teenager or until those horrible last six months. Oh, she tried pot, and maybe shrooms, but never stayed on anything, never got addicted.

Melody had some bad health issues, though. In her 20's she had a lot of trouble with her ears. They were a mess and would swell up and bleed. It was very painful. Local doctors couldn't figure out what was wrong, so they sent her to a teaching hospital up north. They gave her Hydrocodone. Melody also had this pain in her abdomen, pain so severe it would just make her drop to her knees, just out of the blue. They gave her OxyContin, which I know is an opioid. She took them for years.

I found out for sure she was addicted in 2014. When I had knee surgery that year, they gave me OxyContin. Some of it was missing. No one would admit they'd taken it. Melody lied, "You probably miscounted them." But she finally came clean and told me she was addicted to those opioid pills.

John and I were still together then, and Melody and the boys were living with us. Melody was dating a guy; he was in the army. He helped her get off of the opioid pills. He stayed with us for a couple of weeks while he "de-toxed" her. It was terrible. She vomited constantly and had the shakes like I've never seen. I thought she was going to die. But she made it, and I thought, "Thank God, that was behind us."

I went to her doctor and told him to NEVER give her any kind of opioid drugs again. The doctor asked, "Is she in trouble, got a problem?"

I said "Not anymore," and he agreed not to refill her pills.

Melody did those pills, but I knew she'd never do heroin. Most of her friends were guys. She seemed to get along better with them than most girls. Her best friend had died of a heroin overdose. Melody had gone to his dealer and begged him to stop selling to her friend. Melody even went to the police and tried to get the dealer arrested. Her friends meant everything to her, she was true to them.

Melody didn't do any more drugs then, not for a couple of years, maybe until early 2016. She started losing a lot of weight. She said she was working with a doctor, but when I asked about it, the doctor said he had not seen her. I suspected she was doing drugs, taking opioids or other pills, I just didn't know what they were.

I bought a small home in September 2016 and moved out of Lenn's home. I'd finally gotten a little of the money from the divorce settlement. John was enraged that he had to pay me, and took it out on Melody, who was still living with him. John would scream and yell at her, to get a job, to find him some money. She wasn't working, as she'd lost her bartending job.

John figured out how to get some money all right, but it would be the beginning of the end for Melody. Some guys were visiting the house, people Melody knew, and they wanted to cook crack in the house. She said, "No, No Way!!"

But one of them came out of the living room and said, "We are all set here," waving some big bills.

John said, "What I don't see won't hurt me." He was that desperate, because they were going to put him in jail for not paying what he owed me from the divorce. With crack cocaine in the house, Melody was not resisting the temptation any longer. That was the beginning of her end. She was not our Melody anymore; she was in the drug's grip.

I never thought I would have done this, but you do what you have to, to keep your grandchildren safe. And for me, that was getting them away from my daughter. Steve, Melody's oldest, had told me that his Mommy was taking them to a city and leaving them alone. He said, "She'd lock us in the car and then come back after a few minutes." I knew she was going to her dealer and putting those boys in harm's way. I didn't know what else to do, so I called Department of Children and Family Services (DCFS) and turned her in. They took Steve and Corey away from her. It was the hardest thing I'd ever done, but I had to know the boys were safe, not in East St. Louis with her at night, meeting her dealer.

DCFS put Corey in the custody of his father, Jake. But Steve became a DCFS ward. Jake took him, too and kept the boys together. I couldn't have the boys now, not with Melody with me sometimes. But I was fighting for custody of Steve. He was distraught without his Mom and didn't want to be with Jake. He cried, "I just want to be left alone." My heart hurt for him, and Corey, too, without their Mom, but I also knew they were safe.

When Melody learned that DCFS had her kids, she figured out I'd called them. She said she'd never speak to me again and I'd never see the boys again. Of course, she was talking to me in less than a week. Melody just couldn't care for them now; she was too gone on crack. She knew in her heart, though, that I was doing what was best. And that I would be there for her and them, too.

And once the kids were taken, she spiraled down even more quickly. I'm not sure what I expected, perhaps that losing them would scare her into being clean again? It didn't.

In early October 2016, Melody went missing. After the 5th day, we were all so scared. We called the police and made some missing person fliers. I went with some of her friends to East St. Louis looking for her. They knew where she went for her drugs, and thought they might be able to help find her.

I saw her Jeep down a side street and called the police. I started asking people around there and a couple people said they had seen her, and that there were two black girls driving her Jeep. Police found her in an apartment nearby, sleeping. We were waiting near her Jeep and the police brought her back. Melody looked pitiful. She screamed, "Don't touch me!" She didn't even know that she was considered missing and said that someone had given her some real bad stuff, she didn't know what. The police didn't arrest her, since they couldn't prove she'd done anything wrong.

That's when I realized, she couldn't stop the drugs. My Melody was addicted. She didn't have insurance, and no rehab we found would take her, they said they had no bed for her. I just didn't know what to do next. I knew I had to get her away – get her to a new place, where she couldn't get her crack. When she was missing, her best friend, Allie, who lived in Pennsylvania, called. I thought if I got her to Allie, who was not a druggie, she could make it, have a chance, maybe find a rehab center near Allie's. I called Allie and she said, "Come, come now."

Lenn agreed to drive with us, as I hadn't ever driven that far before. Lenn and Melody always had that strange sister relationship where they were on each other's case all the time, but also had each other's back.

When Melody and I went to pick Lenn up the next morning, Melody was ranting and raving, needing her drugs. Lenn said, "No, no way I'm getting in the car with her like that." She refused to go along. So, I headed out by myself with Melody.

A few hours later and she's getting really bad, "Mom, I can't do this. You need to get me drunk or I won't make it," Melody said. So, I stopped and got her a bottle of booze, which she downs in my car as I speed along. Pretty soon, she starts hitting me, grabbing the wheel.

I call Allie in a panic. "Get her some food," she suggested. I did, and finally, Melody falls asleep. But I'm lost. No idea where I am and I didn't know how to use the map on my phone.

I pulled over and found an older couple. They said, "Lady, your phone isn't even on." But they gave me directions.

When Melody woke up a few hours later from being drunk, she said, "Mom, I'm so sorry. Why did you get me that drunk?"

I said, "How did I know how much to get you, I don't drink." We both had a good laugh at that and we finally got to Allie's house.

We found no rehab facility that would take her there, either. We spent five days at Allie's. They smoked pot to help ease Melody's withdrawal symptoms, but no drugs or drinking. On the 5th day, Lenn called and said she'd found a rehab facility in Springfield, IL that would take her sister.

When we got to the rehab in Springfield, Melody begged them to let her in. But their story had changed and they didn't have a bed for her then, so they put her on the waiting list. They said that by mid-November they would have a bed for her.

I thought Melody would die if she didn't get her drugs. I'm not sure why I thought that, I just did. Maybe from that detox episode. I believed that if she didn't get them, she would die. So, I did what I had to, to help keep her alive. Alive until she could get into the rehab center in Springfield. Some days I drove her to her dealer to get her crack. Sometimes in the middle of the night. I'm not proud I did, but you do what you have to, to keep your kid alive. That, and pray and cry a lot.

November came and we went back to the rehab facility in Springfield. Now, they said it would be after Thanksgiving. We went back then and finally, they were going to admit her. In the waiting room, she met two guys who asked, "Are you court-ordered?"

She said, "No." She asked, "What are you in for?"

When they answered, "Heroin," she wouldn't stay. She didn't want anything to do with heroin, even in the facility that could save her.

Melody came back with me, but soon was on the streets, with no real place to live. She lived in the back of a car repair place for a while. On the streets of East St. Louis, her name was "Red." She'd dyed her hair bright red. She'd come to my home from time to time and swear she wouldn't leave, but she always did.

She stole from her dad. She stole $50.00 from a neighbor, and there was a warrant out for her arrest because she failed to appear in court. She even stole her son Steve's Christmas present – his Xbox and games. She was desperate now, needed her drugs, and would do anything to get them.

Crazy, no horrible, shit kept coming her way.

In early 2017 someone kidnapped her. He cut her hair, raped her and threw her naked into the trunk of his car. She begged and kicked to get out. She finally freed herself and ran through the streets of East St. Louis naked, pleading for help. An old man finally let her into his house and called the police. They didn't even take her statement. I think she felt I didn't believe her, so she took me back to the old man's house, so he could corroborate her story.

When I did take her for her drugs, the dealers wouldn't let me see their faces. I never did know any of their names. One dealer finally did, I think he trusted me for some reason. I begged him to please feed her, don't let her die on these streets. He took my phone number and I asked him to let me know when she needed me. He promised he would.

I just didn't know what else to do for her. So many things kept happening that weren't all her fault, she was just in a very bad place.

She kept telling me, "I just can't get off the crack. I can't stop this."

Once she called, desperate, that she needed $50.00 or she was going to get hurt. Lenn went with me to find her. She had no shoes on. I gave her my shoes, but she wouldn't come back with us. Then, I had to drive, but had no shoes, so Lenn gave me hers – she's a thirteen and I'm a size eight. We chuckled about that all the way home.

I'd be sound asleep, and someone would be knocking on my window. I lived alone then for the first time in my life. It would be her. I said, "Melody, why are you knocking on my window at three in the morning?"

She looked at me and said, "Well, I'm sorry, Mom, but the way my life is now this is how I am. I'm up now."

I laughed and said, "But I'm not."

She stole from me just one time. The next week, when she wanted to stay one night, I said, "You can stay, but you will be sleeping with me." (That way, I could hear if she opened the door and was going to steal anything).

She said, "I'm not sleeping with you."

I said, "Then you aren't staying." Needless to say, she slept with me. I also told her if she stole from me ever again, she could never stay and I would have her arrested. She never stole from me again.

John just quit on her after she stole his stuff – he called her "Cracky the clown." So hurtful, she didn't even try to see him after that. I wondered how a father could be that hurtful, could do that. I just couldn't.

Some around her tried to help her and me. One man gave me $100.00 to help get her clean. It just wasn't enough. Another time I convinced her to check into a hospital in St. Louis. I told her, "Tell them you are going to kill yourself, and they will keep you and help you get clean." She wouldn't do it and they didn't keep her.

Melody kept her sense of humor throughout all this. It was one of her best qualities, she could laugh at herself and make light of almost any situation.

Like, every time I went down to East St. Louis to help her, I had to pee. Every time. I'd be nervous and I couldn't make it far or I'd pee on myself. I'm just that age. Ha! Anyway, I would always have to find a deserted side road to squat. She'd get so upset with me, but sometimes we'd laugh because I'd be scared to death being there, no less stopping on a back road to pee.

Once, going home I had to go so bad. She said, "Stop at the Flying J gas station."

I said, "Melody, I can't stop there. I'll pee as soon as I get out of the car." So, I went on those back roads behind there.

She said, "Mom people will see us."

I said, "No one will see us and if they do and want to look at my fat butt that's fine."

She was so nervous. She said, "Mom, this is against the law." I was laughing so hard because here she is doing drugs and I'm sure had a pipe on her somewhere, and she is lecturing me how it's against the law to pee.

Lenn didn't see the humor in Melody's situation, though. She just wouldn't give up hope that she could get her sister back. Lenn made a CD of their life, and I took it to Melody. Melody cleaned up enough after listening to it to have a visit with her boys. DCFS allowed a supervised visit in February 2017, and they were so happy to see her. She had another one arranged the following month, but she had scabies, was covered, so she couldn't see them. By April, Melody was gone.

On April 7, 2017 I got a call from that drug dealer who had promised he would call if Melody needed me. He'd called once before to tell me to quit giving her money, it was the only way to get her to stop. But I didn't do that because I thought she'd die.

Her dealer said, "Are you home? Melody's been in a car wreck."

I asked him, "Is she ok?" I guess he didn't want to tell me on the phone, because he got my address and came to my house. Now, I'm getting scared, right?

When he got there, I first asked him, "Are you going to hurt me?"

He just looked at me really weird, like, "What kind of person do you think I am?" And he told me, "I'm sorry, she is bad, you need to get to St. Louis University Hospital as quick as you can." I later learned that the concerned drug dealer had gotten a call from the ambulance driver, who recognized Melody as someone the dealer knew.

I picked up Lenn and my one close friend, Star, and headed there as fast as we could. I never suspected the nightmare that was ahead of us.

Melody had been in the hospital for a while when we got there. As a "Jane Doe." Even though the person driving the car was in the next ER room, he wouldn't give them her identity. A chaplain met us and told us what he knew about what had happened to her. He said, "There was a high-speed chase between two cars. Melody was in the first one. The driver ran a stop sign and Melody took the brunt of the impact."

She had a big gash in her knee, a shunt was in her head, a broken neck, pelvis and ribs. Her blood pressure was really bad. They suspected Melody had been hiding, down under the dash, when the impact occurred.

It didn't look good for her to make it. I just couldn't believe it, it didn't seem real. We formed a circle and prayed. There wasn't much else for us to do. Just wait and cry. I'm pretty good at the crying part.

We learned over the next few days that Melody had fluid on the brain, and her brain injuries were what they kept calling "massive." I sure hate that word. She was in the hospital for 24 days. She only opened her eyes once, early in her stay, and when they tried to get a response from her, she lifted her middle finger – that's my Melody, feisty to the end.

But no other signs of life emerged. The doctors there were wonderful, but there were so many differing opinions. The trauma team said, "She isn't going to make it."

The neurologist kept saying, "She could heal, but she will not be the same person – not even able to feed herself." I knew Melody would not want that.

Lenn tried to get me to understand what we needed to do after the first week passed. She had seen Melody's CAT scan, and knew we needed to let her go. The chaplain told me, "You will know when it is time." It wasn't time yet. We agree to put a trache in her throat. Later that same day they wanted to give her a feeding tube. That's when I was ready to see the CAT scan. I gasped when I saw it – the whole front of her brain was dead. That's when I decided to let her go. We didn't do the feeding tube.

She was so strong that it took her three days to die. She had such a strong, beautiful heart. They gave her morphine, which I still struggle with. I was by her side the whole time. We all knew the end was coming. I drifted off to sleep for a few minutes and a doctor woke me. "Melody's gone," he said. I think she just wanted to go by herself.

It was May 5th, 2017. Cinco De Mayo day. One of Melody's favorite party days. I am sure she loves that that was her day to go. She died at 4:20 p.m. She'd have loved that time too, since that's the well-known slang in cannabis culture for smoking pot. I think she made that time and date happen. Funny she had that kind of resolve, and still couldn't quit the drugs.

I was asked about donating her organs by a lady. But Melody hadn't signed up as a donor, so I didn't.

The best blessing God gave me through all this was her face. While she was in the hospital her face was all broke out, full of acne and swollen. When I saw her after she had died, her face was like a newborn baby. All clear and perfect. My beautiful girl. God must have done that, to let me see her like that again."

———— // ————

Ann had to stop there for a little while. While she collected herself, I began praying for her. Praying for strength for her, that she could tell me the rest of her story, and marveling at how she ever got through all of that. There was more ahead in her grief journey.

———— // ————

"Lenn made all the arrangements. I just couldn't function, think, help her even. We had Melody cremated. Lenn had big pictures made of some of our favorite photos of Melody and had them on easels. Lenn made a video of Melody's life and we set it to music. I picked the songs. It helped me to have that to do.

After Melody died, I cried and cried. Well, I always was a crier, but this was a different type of crying. I cried so much I couldn't talk. My voice just wouldn't come out. Maybe that was God's work, too, I didn't have to talk to anyone because I couldn't, I could just cry.

Melody had a friend she had been close to since Kindergarten who was a minister. She did the service at a local funeral home. It was so beautiful. Standing room only. There were so many people there that loved her, lots of friends. Friends she was close to before her addiction, friends that meant the world to her.

I just kept thinking how beautiful she was. Not about the last six months where she was a hot mess, an addict, just about all that time before.

Melody had just disappeared those last six months. Most of her friends and our family didn't even know she was an addict, or all of the horrible things that happened to her. And that was ok by me. We were able to say she died in a car accident. But I knew in my heart she died because of the drugs. I think God took her then, in that way, before anything worse could happen to her on the streets.

When someone after the visitation said, "It wasn't a car accident, it was a drug deal gone bad that caused her death," I lit up the Facebook page to let them know that was not true. A mom has to defend her kid even when they are gone, even when you know they were wrong.

The one brother I was closest to died seven months after Melody, which was another huge blow for me. We were close. We worked together and then he was just gone. He lived so generously, maybe to a fault. He had depression and just couldn't get out from under that. He died from alcoholism – just quit eating and went downhill quickly.

My attitude has changed a lot through all of this. I don't care so much about what others think. I used to let others' opinions bother me, but I choose to not let it now. Life is way too short.

I am grateful for the support I got from Lenn, she was so strong, like a rock. And my friend, Star, she was always there for me. I don't know how I'd have made it through the last two years without them.

Lenn was the one that was persistent about getting the guy that was driving charged. She was like a dog with a bone. She went every day to the police station, asking if they'd arrested him yet. We knew who he was – he was in the next bed in the ER when we got there that awful day. The cops hadn't even made a report, so after a couple weeks of this, Lenn went to the District Attorney. That office listened and the guy was eventually arrested and has been in jail since on $200,000 bond. He was charged with a DUI resulting in death and some drug charges, too. The case could take many years. I'm praying it doesn't go to trial, because who knows what will come out about Melody. But I just can't have them plea bargain it down and him not get punished for what he took from us.

I think there are things that need to change to stop all this madness about drugs. I regret not finding a way to get Melody to rehab right away, the first time we knew she was addicted. There should be more beds, more availability so that when an addict is ready, they can go right away.

I also think people on their first offense need to be sent right to counseling and rehab, not prison or just parole. They need help, and we have to find a way to get it for them.

For all those other parents that are struggling with a child, going through this hell, just don't feel bad about what you have to do. Like not giving them money and kicking them out before they steal you blind. I just didn't know what to do.

Another thing is to pray for them. Pray that they will have God's help to recover, to be strong. Prayer can be powerful. I'd say my faith has been jarred, just a little bit, by these last couple of years. It was just so much at one time. I just don't understand why. Why God couldn't just heal her. Or, maybe why He chose not to.

I also think they need to come up with pain killers that aren't addictive. People trust their doctors and take what they give them, never suspecting it will change their lives into a living hell. If Melody would have had other drugs for her ears, maybe she'd never have gone down this path. I don't know if pot is the answer, but maybe.

The thing that's helped me the most is counseling. I found an individual that has been very helpful, and she told me about Heartlinks Addiction Loss Support Group. Going there, being with others who have lived this nightmare, has helped a lot.

I feel like there's not much I haven't been through now. My focus since she died is my grandsons. I thank God every day for

Steve's father relinquishing custody of him to me. He's mine. Just yesterday, Steve caught me crying and I told him, "I'm just missing your mom." Steve made a collage of his mom's pictures, the first outward sign that he's moving forward. He put it right by the one I made for her. It has a poem I wrote with her photo under it.

"You loved the moon

You loved the stars

Now you know

Just where you are"

I have Steve in counseling, too. I just want to help him the best I can. I get to see Corey often, and I work with his dad to be sure the boys stay close. Corey just looks so sad most of the time. That's the hardest part, watching the boys grow up without their mom. They are my reason to go on. This has all been, in a word, sad.

But it's getting better, really. I'm not crying as much, now."

"People cry, not because they are weak. It's because they've been strong for too long."
—Anonymous

Post script: Recently, the family in the story learned that part of the investigation into their daughter's death had been closed. The person driving the car on that fateful day was charged with aggravated DUI resulting in death. He had both alcohol and drugs in his system. He was sentenced to seven years in prison and is required to serve a minimum of six years.

I Laugh to Keep from Crying
– Grief Reflections –
By Diana Cuddeback, LCSW

Ann's story shows the way that living with a loved one struggling with addiction can turn your world upside down. There is an unexplainable kind of craziness that can rule amid fear, love, desperation, and addiction. Unless you have been there, it can be hard to imagine. And remember, there is never a good time to deal with a loved one's addiction. Life does not stop so that the focus can be placed on the addicted person. Managing divorce, young grandchildren, poverty, depression, and homelessness, while also caring for an addicted daughter, presents an overwhelming challenge.

Most people dealing with an addicted loved one come to the experience with little knowledge about substance abuse. Ann is very honest that she did things in order to keep her daughter alive that she never imagined herself doing. She is clear about her lack of knowledge and how it caused her problems. Ann explains, "I thought Melody would die if she didn't get her drugs. I'm not sure why I thought that, I just did."

Ann reminds us to act fast to secure help and to learn about addiction, so that it's possible to make informed choices. She also shows us to **forgive ourselves**: "just don't feel bad about what you have to do," Ann says. This is a powerful suggestion for the **act of self-compassion**. Learning to be gentle with yourself and give yourself kindness as you heal is important.

Ann had so many things happen in her life all at the same time. In order to cope, she had to narrow her world down to only what was most important. She talks about **not listening to other people**.

"My attitude has changed a lot through all of this. I don't care so much about what others think. I used to let others' opinions bother me, but I choose to not let it now. Life is way too short."

This is a challenge, as opinions always mattered to her, but Ann shows us that **grief changes you**. In this very difficult time, Ann focuses on just her grandson. She keeps him safe, even as she is not able to keep her adult daughter, his mother, safe. This **single-minded focus** continues to keep Ann going, as she cares for her grandson even as she grieves.

Professional Counseling and support groups have been a key part of Ann's grief work. Ann had experience with depression, and had a suicide attempt during the process of her divorce. She talks clearly about how helpful medications are for her. Ann's story also highlights something that happens regularly - multiple losses and life crises during an initial grief.

Life does not stop coming at a grieving person. One thing we suggest at Heartlinks Grief Center is to **get small**. By that, we mean that you may have to **do less, go less, be with fewer people, take on less responsibility, and curl up in the fetal position at times when you are grieving**. Being with others takes great energy. A grieving person only has so much energy. A grieving person like Ann, raising a grandchild, dealing with legal issues, and losing a supportive sibling, has even less energy to go around. Ann makes real choices about what she can manage and lets the rest go. She **conserves her energy for what matters most**.

One of the things that Ann did often was **cry**. Crying was a regular and sometimes all-consuming part of her early grief experience:

"After Melody died, I cried and cried. Well, I always was a crier, but this was a different type of crying. I cried so much I couldn't talk. My voice just wouldn't come out. Maybe that was God's work, too, I didn't have to talk to anyone because I couldn't, I could just cry."

Crying is healing. It is also often very irritating, because it can be out of the griever's control to choose when to cry. Crying just happens. Sometimes there is a clear trigger. Sometimes not. Crying for some people is a usual response. For other grieving people, crying is a new and often unwelcome activity.

Be patient with your tears. There is not a lot of research on crying, but some studies have found that tears prompted by emotion - emotional tears - have a different chemical makeup than reflex tears (like tears from a breeze that make your eyes water). Reflex tears are mostly water. Emotional tears have a different chemical makeup, including prolactin (a female hormone), stress hormones (like cortisol, adrenaline and noradrenaline), as well as leucine-enkephalin (an endorphin that relieves pain and improves mood). Science still has a lot to learn about tears, but something about crying is important. Don't overlook **crying as grief tool**.

Perhaps the most striking part of Ann's story is her use of **humor as an anchor** in the midst of craziness. As ill as her daughter became because of her drug use, the two of them used their **humor as a safe connecting place**. Recall the story of an emergency pit stop in a dark and dangerous area on the way to buy drugs. Mother and daughter ended up laughing about legalities - public urination versus purchasing illegal substances.

Ann said, "Melody kept her sense of humor throughout all this. It was one of her best qualities, she could laugh at herself and make light of almost any situation." Ann has that same ability, and uses it to cope with her grief.

CHAPTER SEVEN

A Piece of My Heart

By Ellen Krohne

This is Michael's story, as told by his father, Lenny.

Lenny was the last interview I did for this book. It was a little different from the start. I met him at Mid-America Transplant's offices in St. Louis. All of the other interviews were conducted at Heartlinks Grief Center, where the families were members of the Addiction Loss Support Group. The Mid-America Transplant Foundation partners with Heartlinks Grief Center and provides grant funding to Heartlinks. Heartlinks provides grief support to families, including those who have lost a loved one who was a donor through Mid-America Transplant.

In December 2018, I had gone with Diana, Heartlinks Grief Center Director and co-author of this book, to a partner meeting at Mid-America Transplant Foundation. I was surprised by some of the information we heard, particularly that people who were addicted to drugs could be donors, and asked them if they had a family that would be willing to tell their story. Nicole Kellen, Director of Family and Donor Support Services, said she would ask, and called me several weeks later to set a date for the interview.

Lenny shakes my hand firmly when Nicole introduces me, then leans in and gives me a hug. "I'm a hugger, he laughs nervously."

"That's ok, I am, too," I respond, also nervous.

He says, "My given name is Leonard, but my friends call me Lenny. Call me Lenny."

As we settle into the conference room chairs across from each other, I notice Lenny's eyes filling up with tears before we even start talking. "I'm not the person I was before. I've changed since we lost Michael. Now I want to help others, help ease their pain, but it's selfish, because it helps me more," he says, as his story begins.

———— // ————

"I'm the youngest of five, with two brothers and two sisters. And if you couldn't tell, I'm a full-blooded Italian. And proud to be. I was raised right by my parents, Louis and Vita. Right by them means Catholic and all that goes with that. You know - mass, statues, Hail Mary's and the belief that He will always be there, always make it right.

Right by them meant that people would say about their son, "What a fine man." And I always was that man before. I was the strong one, praying for others. Now, I'm so tired of hearing, "I'll pray for you." I'm supposed to be that strong guy praying for others.

But I'm not anymore.

I graduated from Riverview Gardens High School in 1979, a big, public high school in St. Louis. People smoked pot and drank some. I never did more than that.

I got married young, and we had three boys. My father, Louis, was elderly and I wanted to marry before he passed. Louis, named after my father, was born in 1984, Michael was born in 1987, and Anthony in 1990. They were three peas in a pod. Great boys, so much fun, those little string beans.

My father passed away in 1988. He got to meet his namesake, Louis, and Michael, too. It is special to me that he got to know them.

My wife and I divorced in 1993. It was my fault, but I don't regret it. I met the person I was meant to spend the rest of my life with, Shannon. My soulmate. The one who completes me. And we've been together ever since, having two more sons. The five boys treated each other well, grew up together.

At the time of the divorce, I was 27. I was a business owner, powerful, and I felt I had everything in my control. I could manage it all. Then my ex-wife moved the boys to the Lake of the Ozarks and I was powerless to stop her. I hadn't expected that.

Now I was a long-distance dad. Not something I wanted, but we did the best we could. I was no deadbeat dad. I never missed a weekend with them. I spent as much time as I could, and worked hard at keeping a foot in the door. In hindsight, it may not have been enough. You want to have those conversations with them in that little window of time you have them. Important conversations where you focused 125% of your attention and presence, and kids, they give you 10% of their attention. I just hope some things sank in – I believe they did. But I know the divorce was hard on them.

Michael graduated from Camdenton High School in 2006. He was just a beautiful boy. He smiled from the bottom of his heart. And a good boy. Spotless. One my mother was proud to say was her grandson. She loved and nurtured and helped to raise our little Michael until she passed in 2004.

Michael was smart, so smart. And athletic. He was so flexible; his body was like a spring. It was a joy to watch him play sports. I was his soccer coach before they moved to the Lake of the Ozarks.

When Michael was around ten years old, he asked if he could play ice hockey. I was always a big hockey fan, a loyal Blues supporter, and I was proud he wanted to play. I split the difference in distance between our homes with my ex-wife, and he played in Jefferson City, Missouri for the Capitals. And he was good. He was a little guy, the shortest on the team by eight inches. They elected him Captain anyway. Their team won it all that last year – he made me so proud, holding up that trophy with the "C" for Captain on his chest.

His real passion, though, was golf. And he was a star. An exceptional technical golfer. After a year at the University of Missouri he went to the San Diego Golf Academy. He was good, but to make it as a professional you had to be even better than he was. After a year he transferred back to Lindenwood University in St. Charles, Missouri and earned his degree in finance. His graduation day is one of my best memories.

While he was in San Diego, we got to go to Torrey Pines, the fabulous golf course on the ocean, for a tournament. Tiger Woods was his idol, and we saw him play. It was Father's Day, and I remember being there with him, looking out over the beautiful expanse of blue water and saying to him, "Michael, how did we get here? Not much better than this, in this world." And him smiling back at me with that beautiful smile.

I stayed with him that weekend at his fraternity house – a fantastic home, worth millions. There were two or three of his friends I really didn't like. But I didn't say that then. They all drank beer, partied, but I didn't know of anything else, any drugs.

Anthony, Michael's younger brother, also visited Michael in San Diego. Anthony told me they went across the border into Mexico to get pills (maybe opioids, I'm not sure) a few times. I wonder now if that was a stepping stone to other drugs.

Anthony always could relate best to Michael. They had a strong, brotherly bond. All three boys moved back to the St. Louis area when they came of age. I didn't meddle in their lives, though. That wasn't my place, they were men by then.

Michael worked at a large real estate firm after he got his degree. In late 2015, Michael came to work with me. I'd bought a used car lot, and Michael came on as my Finance Manager. I saw him every day those last months, which I hold as a blessing. I know in my heart he wasn't using drugs when we worked together.

On February 18th 2016 I got a call very early one morning. "This is St. Joseph's Hospital. We have your son. He is still alive. You need to come now."

In shock, I screamed, "What happened?"

The person on the other end of the phone said calmly, "A drug overdose."

My mind immediately went to Anthony. The middle child of our five, he'd had some issues over the years and I thought perhaps he'd gotten into some trouble. No, they said, "It is your son, Michael."

So many things ran through my mind as I raced to the hospital. Michael was on the way to being engaged, doing fine. Sure, he was "on the outs" with her right now, but it just didn't make sense. I'd just seen him at work the week before. There had to be some mistake, they were wrong. It just could not be that he used drugs.

I got to the hospital and learned he'd been out with a group of guys, just a "night out with the boys." Someone had bought heroin. Only it turned out not to be heroin at all, it was Fentanyl. Don't get me wrong, he should in no way have used drugs, but I know in my heart he didn't know that what he was taking would kill him. Michael always did feel he was invincible.

He was wrong.

I believe the guys he was with, not sure what to do, waited too long to call the ambulance. By the time the paramedics arrived and administered Narcan, it was too late, he was too far gone. Narcan doesn't work that well on Fentanyl anyway, like it does on heroin, but they didn't know then that it wasn't heroin.

The police were at the hospital, too, and they were just plain rude. "This happens every day," one of them said. To them this was just one more drug addict that had overdosed. They didn't even try to find the dealer that sold the guys the Fentanyl.

Michael had a faint pulse, and that was about all. They told us he was brain dead. He laid there like that, just no response. Hooked up to all kinds of machines. Tore me apart, seeing my boy like that. The doctors tried to revive him, and we tortured ourselves about what to do for ten days. They tried everything. They'd cool him down and heat him back up, over and over. But nothing worked.

People tried to help us make the decision to turn off the machines. But it was his mother and I that took that responsibility, no one else. I knew at day three, but it felt like carrying a car, it was so hard to actually turn them off, knowing he'd really be gone. I still question myself. Would it be better to have him here to talk to, to visit, even if he weren't really there?

The Catholic liaison at the hospital kept talking to us about the sanctity of life and extraordinary measures. My Catholic beliefs kept me praying for a miracle.

And people that loved him kept coming to see him. Lots of girls, maybe some past girlfriends, I think, sobbing, crying. He had so many friends, and it made me proud to have so many come to visit him. And harder to make the decision.

As I prayed for guidance on what to do, a woman came up to me with a form. She said her name was Julie with Mid-America Transplant. I thought she was asking for a donation, and my Italian temper flared. I have to admit, I was at my wit's end. My nerves were shot and I was less than respectful at that point.

Julie calmly said, "I have a form here that Michael had signed a few months ago that I'd like to talk with you about. Michael signed up to be an organ donor."

Suddenly, Julie became an angel. In the midst of so much that was bad, this one thing was good. It wasn't a decision we had to make. Michael had taken care of this; it was his wish to be a donor – to give the gift of life to others.

We slowly realized that he could do so much good. And Julie was just wonderful, explaining everything that was ahead. She was special.

My ex-wife and I made the decision to turn off life support the next day, February 29th. Michael was gone the following day, March 1st, 2016. We learned later that 35 people were recipients of his donation, both organs and tissue. I cling to that - 35 people that he helped. We got a letter from Mid-America Transplant on the recipients, and it was two pages long. That part makes me feel good, proud of Michael one more time.

I am blessed to have a life-long best friend, Chris. He helped us make the funeral arrangements. I should more accurately say he made them. Oh, I was at the funeral home, but only my body. My mind was in a daze, numb. Michael was cremated and I bought urns for everyone, so each of his family could always have him near. I don't think I'd have gotten through those days without Chris.

We had a memorial gathering for him in St. Charles, at the funeral home there, on March 5th. It started late morning and went until three, concluding with a service. The outpouring of love filled my heart. To see so many people, I bet 500 or more came. They had to open all four parlors for the service. His four brothers and I standing together. I think we must have looked like idiots, just all five of us standing there bawling. There was just face upon face upon face, flashing a foot away from mine. "I'm so sorry." "My condolences." Over and over. Some just stared and couldn't say anything. Some people said hurtful things, I've blocked those out. If I said anything, I don't remember what it was. I was doing my best to control a day I had no control over.

People were kind enough not to ask, "How did he die?" I think friends had told everyone there. I didn't say it out loud, still have trouble even thinking, "My son Michael Leonard Tocco died of a drug overdose." I don't know if I ever will be able to say those words."

———⁄⁄———

Leonard has been choked up and tearful as we talk. But he breaks into a beautiful smile from time to time, when he remembers Michael. He continues, sharing his grief journey.

———⁄⁄———

"Before you know it, it's back to life. Back to work, to eating and sleeping, to normal living. But not for me. I stand here today just a shell of who I was before Michael's death. It's been three years almost, and some days I'm still a mess. I keep going back to those days Michael laid in that hospital. I wonder if I'll still be stuck here ten years from now.

I played the blame game for a while. Looking back, these were "knee-jerk" feelings, certainly none of them the cause of Michael's action. I blamed the dealer that sold them the Fentanyl, blamed the friends he was with for not acting quickly, blamed his girlfriend for their struggles. I blamed Michael for being ignorant of the dangers in doing drugs, thinking he could just do that and be ok. Always thinking he was invincible. Lots of bitter blame. And still he's dead.

Lots of blame mixed in with a load of guilt. Guilt that I wasn't a better dad, that I wasn't around more. Just crushing guilt.

And, in ways, embarrassed. Embarrassed to have drugs associated with our family name, our heritage. I will never know if he used drugs before that night. If he did, I'm embarrassed that he would be so foolish, to throw away his life for drugs. And I believe some people think less of him and me because he died this way.

My niece, Mary Jo, sent me this saying, "Adult children are not a reflection of their parents, they are a reflection of their choices." It was nice to get, affirming, but it hasn't helped my guilt for Michael's death.

I cherish my brothers and sisters. They are my go-to. They have been there for me, and I know they always will be. They know I'm not fun now, and they love me anyway. When I laugh and have fun, even now almost three years later, I feel guilty.

The other rock in my life has been my wife, Shannon. She understands me, my struggles with this pain. She can talk about

Michael's death, where I can't yet. I'm not sure if I'd have made it through this without her. We talk about the good times, that helps.

I've learned a lot. About myself and others, too. I've learned who my real friends are. Hell of a way to find out, but I know now. Those real, true friends that have stuck with me, they are now family. When I see these friends, I hug and kiss them. They know why.

The day after the funeral, I was done in, I just couldn't lift my head from my pillow. I heard the doorbell ring, and when I finally answered it, there were just flowers on the porch. I read the front of the card, it said, "We know exactly how you feel." I had a guttural reaction, just anger at the thought that anyone could think they knew my pain, and threw the flowers to the floor. Sobbing, I went back upstairs to my fetal position. The next day I read the card; the flowers were from, Mike and Lisa, and I was aghast at my terrible reaction. Thank God, my apology for trashing their gift was accepted graciously. These neighbors - no much more - true friends - their son hung himself in his bedroom. They didn't know my pain exactly, but they did know the pain of losing a child.

Another close friend, at the funeral home mind you, said, "I could never burn my kid." That hurt me badly. We struggled with what Michael would have wanted. We'd never discussed his funeral preferences with him, right? A year later, her child who had a long-term illness died and they had him cremated. She remembered saying that to me and apologized, saying, "I can't believe I said that, I'm so sorry." I have learned that people don't know what to say when someone dies, especially of a drug overdose, so they sometimes say things that are hurtful, not really meaning them. I'm blessed that she and her husband are such great friends, and I was able to let it go.

This couple is "in the group" now, too – the small group that really needs each other but that no one wants to join. That group of friends that have lost a child. Mike and Lisa, my forgiving neighbors who lost their son to suicide, they are in the group, too. We get together from time to time to just be together. That group is close family.

I cherish those things that people have given me to remember Michael. One friend gave me a tree, another a stone for our garden, a third a brick with his birth and death dates. Those gifts mean a lot to me. Probably that Catholic upbringing – we need those concrete symbols.

I started journaling about a month after he died. I write to Michael. Just about things I'm feeling and things that are happening. I've eaten ice cream every night for most of my life. One of my passions. About a month after he died, I wrote in my journal, "I hope I choke and die if I eat another bite." I haven't eaten any ice cream since then. I'm not sure why this makes me feel better, but in some strange way, it does.

Since Michael died, I am trying hard to be a better person – to not get mad or hold vengeance. I apologize more and speak kinder words. You never know when they will be your last. I'm not perfect at this, that's for sure, but I'm more thoughtful about what I say and do, and am consciously trying.

My focus now is on trying to do good. I believe Michael is in heaven, watching. I need to focus on honoring him, his memory. Focus on ways to help others through this. And here's that selfish part. When I'm doing that, helping others, I can talk about him, let it go. Otherwise, I just can't. So, it helps me more than anything.

It took me a few more months to realize I needed to "do something." I built a bench. It was a labor of love and helped me to heal. As I sawed the wood and sanded it smooth, I poured my love for Michael and my pain into every stroke. I took it to his childhood golf course and we had a ceremony – a big reveal with our family.

I started drawing, too. I've always liked to draw, to create things, but this time I'm doing it with meaning. I just have this feeling like a piece of my heart is ripped out. So, I drew that. It was the inspiration for the foundation I've started, "Piece of My Heart Foundation."

I want to help others' pain. I want to make a difference now in the years I have left on this earth. I want Michael's death to make a difference to others. We had the foundation organized by the end of 2016. It was important to me to start it in the year he died.

The Piece of My Heart Foundation donates to help parents and families that have lost a child. The purpose of the Foundation is, "Helping parents and families cope with the loss of a child." Everything the Foundation and its supporters do is in honor of Michael. We've done golf tournaments to raise funds. That felt natural, since Michael loved the game so much. A huge success. When I left that night after the first golf event, after all the hard work of the tournament, I felt better. Like I had let go of a little of that pain. Next, we are planning a Trivia Night.

With some funds available for the Foundation, we started a scholarship at the Camdenton High School, where Michael graduated. We had more than 30 applicants and it was amazing that the one we chose through an anonymous application process looked so much like Michael when he accepted the award. My heart healed a little bit more then, too.

We give donations of money to those that have lost a child and need help. A young mother lost her daughter who had Downs Syndrome, and we helped her. Another child had MS and died and we donated to that family, too. Small amounts that we hope can let them know someone cares.

The Piece of My Heart Foundation partners with Mid-America Transplant. You never ask your child, "What charity would you be interested in?" But that part was made clear because of Michael's enrolling in organ donation to "Give the Gift of Life" to those in need. We are proud to partner with them, and made a donation to the Mid-America Transplant Foundation at Christmas. They provide solace to me as I've journeyed through these last three years. I participate in Mid-America Transplant Foundation events, like the 5K run. Sometimes I cry when I do these things, but I'm trying to find that spot where I can help others. But really, participating helps me more.

The Piece of My Heart Foundation also provides gas cards and movie tickets for those waiting in the Mid-America Transplant Recipient Wing. People stay there, just waiting for a donor. The

Recipient Wing is a little like I feel most of the time. The people there are just a shell, waiting for healing, waiting for a part, maybe a heart, while the world goes on around them.

The only advice I can give to others struggling with this journey is to hold on to your family unit the best you can. Keep your kids close.

And realize that the loved one that is dead is not the only casualty in this epidemic. The entire family is thrown off, out of whack, when you lose a precious member. Michael's younger brother, Anthony, needs Michael. He always looked to him for guidance and advice, and he is struggling now because Michael isn't here for him. Breaks my heart.

I don't think there is anything I can do to stop this opioid crisis. It's too big for me to figure out. Maybe too big for anyone to figure out. Although I pray we can.

A piece of my heart is gone, yet I feel my faith is stronger. I'm praying my ass off. He just doesn't answer too often. Or perhaps I'm praying for Him to make this right, and there is no answer I can understand.

I feel like I'm just a thread in a rug. A small, small piece of a big world. I just want to do the rest of my days right. Help others through the Piece of My Heart Foundation. And feel Michael smile down on me from heaven."

A Piece of My Heart
– Grief Reflections –
By Diana Cuddeback, LCSW

Lenny's story of Michael's overdose death focuses on another way an addiction-related loss can leave loved ones grieving: with disbelief and surprise, a shocking event dropped into the life of a family completely unexpectedly. Lenny's brutal honesty and willingness to share his experience provides the gift of many grief teachings.

Lenny movingly describes the **numbness** that is a regular part of the grief process. It can be particularly strong where loss comes unexpectedly and suddenly, or if there has been a long and exhausting period before loss. For a father taken completely by surprise at his son's drug use, let alone his overdose-induced death, numbness seems like a protective emotion for an overwhelmed brain. **Understanding the beneficial quality of numbness** in the grief process is important. One must navigate many challenges, activities, and rituals when the death of a loved one occurs. When a death is unexpected, or out of sync with a grieving person's knowledge, belief and expectations of life, the brain struggles to catch up with reality. Numbness can be a brief resting spot. Numbness can help people get through the rituals and actions that feel impossible to accomplish. Lenny explains it like this: "Oh, I was at the funeral home, but only my body. My mind was in a daze, numb."

Ride the numb is a suggestion we often pass along at Heartlinks Grief Center. People describe the numbness as a feeling of emptiness or grayness, where they feel blank. Of course, a person can't stay forever in a grief-numbed state. Numbness is a cushion for grief, particularly early grief, but not a permanent solution. People often feel their move out of numbness intensely and must seek ways to manage the pain that comes when that numbness wears off. Getting stuck in the numbness is another grief difficulty entirely, and more than we can handle here.

Lenny explains about managing the grief process as he moves out of numbness. "Before you know it, it's back to life. Back to work, to eating and sleeping, to normal living. But not for me. I stand here today just a shell of who I was before Michael's death." And from this point of devastation, Lenny finds ways to deal with his grief and create a new sort of connection with his deceased son.

Lenny talks about the **hope that donating Michael's organs and tissues brought** to him and to Michael's mother. He explains that Michael's documented choice to donate his organs relieved a burden of decision from his shoulders. Lenny feels pride in Michael's decision and the 35 people touched by these donated gifts. Lenny feels a connection to the organ procurement organization, staff, and other donor families, which gives him a sense of relationship and community.

Lenny's charity, The Piece of My Heart Foundation, **honors his son by helping others**. Lenny says of this work, "I want to lessen others' pain – I want to make a difference now in the years I have left on this earth. I want Michael's death to make a difference to others." He explains that the hard work of fundraising lets him, "let go a little of that pain." He says that the opportunity to help others helps him to feel that, "my heart healed a little bit more then, too."

Finding a way to maintain a connection with a lost loved one is a positive way to care for yourself when you are grieving. The idea of closure was mentioned earlier as a generally non-useful idea. Instead of closing the relationship off, maintaining a connection with a deceased love one can help. Finding activities, like Lenny's fundraising, keeps him moving and connecting with the present world while maintaining a bond with his son. These **continuing bonds are a healing grief strategy**. And what does that look like? Lenny describes it perfectly, "I just want to do the rest of my days right. Help others through the Piece of My Heart Foundation. And feel Michael smile down on me from heaven."

Before we move to the next story, here are a few more ideas that Lenny shares. Lenny talks about the importance of expression in his grief process. He mentions **expression through prayer, journaling, drawing and building**. All of these activities are great ideas. And no one told Lenny these things, he just listened to the push inside of him, the push to move the pain inside to the outside through many different forms of expression. **Grieving people have great wisdom inside them**. Listening to it and acting upon it are critical.

And finally, for those of you supporting grieving people, Lenny's story illustrates many things that you can do. **Be there**. **Provide concrete help** (like his friend helping with funeral arrangements). **Show up**. A big turnout at bedside or at a funeral soothes grieving people with the knowledge that their child is important to others.

Give **concrete items of remembrance** if these are useful to the grieving family. You may have to ask first if you are not sure. If **you say something stupid, apologize**. Sometimes in trying to help we make things worse. **Be willing to go back and make amends**. If you don't catch it right away, but you notice tension in the relationship, ask later. Don't ask if you don't want a real answer. Lenny's friendship with one person was lost due to an insensitive comment, but then reestablished when she had a loss that made her rethink her comment. She owned her mistake, Lenny accepted her apology, and the friendship was transformed for all parties.

The Gift of Hope and Healing
By Mid-America Transplant's Communications Department

The information for this part of the chapter was provided by Mid-America Transplant to explain organ and tissue donation and how to register to become a donor.

Please note this information is specific to the region served by Mid-America Transplant. Similar facilities are in operation across the United States and the one in your region can be found at *www.organdonor.gov*.

Anyone nationwide can sign up on the National Organ Donor Registry at *www.registerme.org*.

Who is Mid-America Transplant?

Mid-America Transplant saves lives through organ and tissue donation. We work across the Midwest, serving counties throughout eastern and southern Missouri, southern Illinois, and northeast Arkansas.

As an organ and tissue procurement organization, our work happens at the intersection of life and death. We help donor families through moments of grief and loss, facilitate organ and tissue donations for transplant, and support transplant patients.

Who is eligible to donate organs and tissues?

In the U.S., any adult can sign up to be an organ and tissue donor. In some states, people under the age of 18 can commit to donation, but authorization by a parent or guardian is generally required for underage individuals who have passed away.

Even if you have a medical condition, there is still a chance that you can donate. For example, organs from a donor with HIV can be transplanted to a patient who is also HIV positive. Individuals who died of a drug overdose are also eligible to donate. If a patient is unable to donate organs because of a preexisting condition or the cause of death, they may still be able to donate gifts of tissue.

What is the difference between organ and tissue donation?

Gifts of organ and tissue donation can make an incredible difference for patients awaiting transplant. For organ donation, one donor can save up to eight lives through gifts of heart, kidney, pancreas, lung, liver, and intestines. These gifts mean the world to patients who are waiting for a lifesaving transplant.

A tissue donor can heal up to 75 people through gifts of cornea, skin, heart valves, bone, blood vessels, and connective tissue. These gifts can help patients with severe burns, vision-threatening disease, or ligament damage.

Each year, approximately 35,000 organ transplants and 1.75 million tissue transplants bring renewed life to patients and their families.

Who pays for organ and tissue donation?

The transplant recipient pays for the costs related to donation, typically through insurance, Medicare, or Medicaid. The donor family is only responsible for the cost of their loved one's medical care and funeral services.

What does it mean to register as an organ or tissue donor?

Registering usually takes place years before donation happens, but it is an important step towards someday saving lives. In the event of your death, your registration as a donor will let your family know your final decision. This choice can also bring healing to the people you leave behind, who will know that you helped others through the gift of donation.

When a person dies, how does the donation process work?

For a person to become an organ donor, he or she has to die in a very specific way. Usually, people who are able to donate organs pass away after accidents, aneurysms, or strokes. Most people, no matter how they die, can be potential tissue donors. Suitability for organ and tissue donation is determined at the time of death.

Doctors do everything they can to save the patient's life, but if the injuries are too severe, the hospital will contact a local organ and tissue procurement organization such as Mid-America Transplant.

A representative from our team will check to see whether the patient registered as an organ and tissue donor. If they did sign up, that serves as legal consent for donation. If the patient did not sign up, a member of our staff will talk to the donor family about the decision to donate. Our team is compassionate and genuinely cares for families who are coping with an incredible loss. We not only help them navigate the donation decision, we are also truly there for them for as long as they need us. Whether families are looking for a counseling referral, information about grief, or someone to talk to on a difficult day, our donor family support team can help.

If donation is authorized, our team will begin a health evaluation, looking at the patient's medical and social history. This information will determine whether the individual is a candidate for organ or tissue donation, or both.

Once the family members have said their final goodbyes at the hospital, the donor is transferred to our facility, where they are treated with gratitude and respect. Families often have special requests for the recovery process, and our team takes those decisions very seriously. This could mean reading a letter from loved ones, playing a favorite song, or holding the donor's hand.

With an onsite laboratory, we can perform high-quality tests right in our own facility. Our technicians carefully check for infectious disease and safely match donors with potential recipients. Organs are matched to patients based on a number of factors, including blood and tissue typing, medical need, time on the waiting list, and geographical location. If a donation is matched and accepted by the surgeon, it will be transported to the transplant center as soon as possible. While organ transplants typically happen just hours after recovery, the gift of tissue can be preserved for up to five years.

In the weeks that follow donation, we provide the family with information on the lives their loved one was able to save. We also reach out with resources related to grief and loss, including counseling referrals, educational materials, and invitations to remembrance events.

As part of our commitment to donor families, Mid-America Transplant supports several grief centers across the region, including Heartlinks Grief Center. We rely on these partners to provide professional counseling services and other resources to families who are struggling with grief.

How easy is it to sign up?

The easiest way to sign up is to visit the National Organ Donor Registry at *www.registerme.org*. It takes less than five minutes to register as an organ donor to give the gift of hope and healing.

CHAPTER EIGHT

Things Won't Ever Be the Same
By Ellen Krohne

This is Eric's story, as told by his mother, Laura.

I fight back the tears that I can feel coming as Laura starts to tell me about her son. Born on December 18, 1985, Eric was her middle child. Eric was such a calm baby, even in utero, she laughs.

Calm, but he was born to be a soldier – what she knew he would be. He never crawled like regular infants. Eric did that one-arm crawl of an army man. He was fascinated with guns, with war, with battles, and that's all he played as a little boy. He'd make a gun out of anything – a stick, a fork.

He was enamored with the Civil War and learning all about it. When it was his turn to choose a family vacation spot, he chose Gettysburg. He was so knowledgeable that in 5th Grade his teacher let him teach the class on the Civil War. He was that kind of kid; smart, determined and so curious that he'd question and dig until he understood all there was to know about a subject.

My tears are because our son is the same age, born in September 1985, and as Laura talks I realize that I could easily be sitting in her seat. Our son, too, begged to enlist in the military after 9-11, only we didn't let him. She did, and the consequences she's had to endure are the hardest I can imagine, losing a child. Losing a child in the way that she lost Eric; I cannot even imagine what hell she has gone through.

She begins his story calmly, slowly, as those ten long years ago when she lost him at just 23 years old come flooding back.

—————//—————

"Eric was born at Great Lakes Naval Station. The view outside my window while I was in labor with him was a winter wonderland; snow heavy on the trees and covering the lake, it was just beautiful. Like Eric. My husband was in the Navy and we were stationed at Great Lakes when he was born. Maybe that started his fascination with being a soldier. Maybe he was just born with it.

My husband and I met at Southern Illinois University Edwardsville. He went to dental school and I graduated with a degree in biology. We married in 1982 and quickly had our first son in 1984, and then Eric 18 months later. The Navy transferred us from Great Lakes to Newport News, VA. When my husband got out of the Navy we moved to O'Fallon, IL and he bought a dental practice in St. Louis. It was 1991.

We were a busy, happy family. Both boys had many friends at school and participated in sports. We were blessed with one more child, Mary, in 1998. I've always called her our gift from heaven. Eric was my helper with the new baby. He was so gentle and sweet, excited to have a little sister.

Eric was outgoing and such a happy kid, willing to tackle and learn anything. When his friend talked of starting a band,

Eric wanted to be a part of it, so we got him a guitar. He taught himself and we quickly realized that he had a gift for playing. The band, named 50/50, did well and suddenly he was traveling, and young girls were screaming my young teenager's name. They even recorded some songs. One favorite of mine was "Things Won't Ever Be the Same." Those words that Eric sang come back and haunt me now.

Then the day came that changed everything. September 11, 2001. It hit Eric hard. He had a solid streak of patriotism in him. Solid like no one else I knew. All he could talk about was enlisting, helping, doing something, doing his duty.

He was 15.

A big NO, that's what we told him at 15. When he graduated early from O'Fallon High School in December, 2003, we begged him to go on to college. Then, if he still wanted to enlist, he could, and he'd enter as an officer. But that's not what he wanted. He wanted to fight, to be a soldier, to be a Marine, to "fight with the best."

He was so patriotic and so idealistic. From his years of studying war and soldiers, he had a view in his head of how soldiers stuck together, took care of each other no matter what. His idealism met reality soon after he enlisted.

I regret a few points along the path to Eric's destruction, and signing the paper for him to enlist at 17 is one of them. I did it because he was so persistent, so sure that's what he wanted. I didn't want to stand in the way of his dream, his destiny. The war in Iraq seemed to me to be a distant conflict.

I believe if my Dad had still been alive, it would have been different. He had fought in World War II and had a different, not idealistic, view of war. He'd insisted that my brothers stay in college during the Vietnam War draft, helping ensure they wouldn't get drafted.

But Dad wasn't there to talk our patriotic son out of going. Eric went to Camp Pendleton in January, 2004 for boot camp. We all went to his graduation ceremony in April and cried, including Eric. He stood on the parade ground and cried, he was so full of pride and honored to be a Marine.

He went for further training as an infantryman, a mortarman specifically, after graduation and was assigned to the 1st Battalion, 1st Regime, 1st Marine Division. Called the First of the First, it is the "old guard" of the service.

By that time the war in Iraq was raging, and in December, 2004 Eric got his orders and was deployed to Iraq. But as fate would have it, his ship was first diverted to Sri Lanka for help with the tsunami that hit that country on December 26, 2004. Eric and his fellow marines were enlisted to help with cleanup efforts. I remember him saying, "Mom, there are so many dead kids." It just took him aback. I don't think he was prepared for that kind of service. He never talked to me about his experiences in Iraq, although I know from his friends whom he did talk with that the killing tore him apart. But he did tell me about those dead kids.

Eric was also disillusioned about his fellow soldiers in the unit. There was some camaraderie, but not at all like he expected. There was a lot of treating each other disrespectfully and stealing from each other. They weren't equipped, as he thought they would be, with the best of everything. No, instead they lacked supplies and even food and water at times on the battlefield. The realities of war.

I remember him calling me once, I was in Kohl's trying on jeans. I'd just gotten a cell phone. It was Eric calling, from Iraq. He was using the interpreter's phone to call me, as they were going on a mission. He said, "They took our hand guns, we don't have the right body armor or supplies." He was panicked. And so was I. A world away and no way to help him – I just froze there in that dressing room. It was a horrible, defeated feeling.

He'd call and talk about his team not supporting each other, stealing from each other. His idealistic view was shattered. I believe that he started doing drugs then. I'm not sure what kind. Maybe pills or morphine, I'm not sure.

My Grandma Julie had a prayer she said when her son, my Dad, was in WW II and I said it daily, sometimes more than once. It gave me strength and I hoped it would protect my soldier son:

"Holy Mary, Mother Immaculate, hear my earnest plea. Protect and guard my soldier son, take care of him for me. When danger stalks too close to him, his hand in yours do take, and lead him to a place secure, my boy do not forsake. But most of all, dear Mother mine, his soul I trust to thee. That grace sublime in him may shine and God-like he may be."

He finally got sent home from Iraq in June, 2005 and had a month of leave. I was so grateful my prayers had been answered and he came home uninjured. I soon realized that while he was not shot in the war, he had been gravely wounded.

I just wanted him to be home with us and spend time with us. He seemed so distant, not the boy we'd known. He spent much of the month sleeping at his friend, TJ's, house. I was so naïve, I didn't have any experience with drugs, but should have known that's one of the signs – sleeping for extended periods. Eric said his paycheck had been stolen. I realize now where it went.

Eric went to San Diego to the Marine base after his leave. It's funny, but I remember just where I was when I'd get these calls from him. I was in Schnucks when he called me. "Mom, are you busy?"

"I'm just going in to get some groceries, what's up?"

"Oh, nothing, I can call back later," he said. But I could tell something was very wrong by the tone of his voice. We had that kind of connection.

"No, we can talk now," I said.

"I'm in the hospital, Mom." My knees buckled. Every horrible thing that could have happened to him raced through my mind.

Then he said, "I'm in the psych ward, Mom." One thing I never imagined. And my world tumbled apart.

He'd been in a training exercise and had pulled a gun on a fellow soldier. Just totally lost it. Luckily, no one was hurt or it would have been much worse. He was diagnosed with Post Traumatic Stress Disorder (PTSD).

My son, my beautiful, determined boy, was in a psych ward. I just couldn't fathom this. I flew out immediately. They let me see him but didn't give me much information. I spent a week with him and I know it sounds weird, but it was a wonderful week. They let me take him out of the hospital and we went to the San Diego Zoo, went to have dinners together. Just spent some good time together that I'll always treasure.

Everywhere on the streets of sunny San Diego are homeless people. Eric, always big-hearted to those less fortunate, would stop and talk with each of them a little while, give them something.

He didn't seem sick to me. Then, one morning I arrived later than I'd planned to and he was distraught. Panicked. And I began to see what the doctors saw. I knew things really weren't right with Eric.

They kept him in the hospital for three months. They had a protocol to follow for treatment. He was honorably discharged in November 2005 and came home. And the nightmare began.

His behavior when he came home was irrational. He was irritable, didn't sleep or slept all the time, acted recklessly. He was on edge all the time, angry. We attributed all this behavior to the PTSD.

Eric received a small severance from the Marines – five or six thousand dollars, I think. I asked him after he was home a few weeks if he wanted to look for a car or get an apartment with the money. He said, "Mom, I don't have that money."

"What do you mean, you don't have it?"

He said, just matter-of-factly, "Mom, I spent it on drugs. I'm an addict."

It felt like when he was a toddler and he'd make up words. His own language – DeDe was Thank you, Zeboken was something he said all the time and we never did know what it meant. Surely, "I'm an addict" didn't mean he was using drugs.

"No, you're not," I told him. I just couldn't believe what he was telling me.

Slowly, I started to wrap my head around the words – "I'm an addict." We talked through all the W questions – Why? Where do you get it? What do you use? We had that kind of rapport – I didn't panic as he told me, just listened dumbstruck at what he was telling me.

He told me how cocaine was his drug of choice and it was readily available. How he didn't use needles, so don't worry about that. How it helped block the pain of his memories from the war. How all the money he had went to his dealer.

As I've mentioned, I've got several points of regret along Eric's journey, and two are here. One is that I didn't tell Eric's father for a few months. And I think I was in denial, too, that this could really be Eric's reality, could have happened to our family, to us. I just didn't know how to tell his father that his son was a drug addict.

The second regret is that I didn't act aggressively to get him into treatment. I thought, Eric and I can solve this – I can figure out how to get him to quit. I had no idea how hard withdrawal is or what that even meant. I was in denial.

Pretty soon, things started going missing. First, my Rolex watch. Eric denied he'd taken it – but it was at a pawn shop where he'd sold it. I started sleeping with my wallet and rings under my pillow. Stealing was no big thing to him. Or lying. He did what he needed to do to get his drugs. I didn't know how to cope with the irrational ways he was acting or where to turn for help.

Eric was playing in a rock band with his friends again and going to Southwestern Illinois Community College in our hometown. I was trying to pretend he was normal, not an addict, just our Eric. I got a call that he'd stolen an energy drink from the cafeteria at school. Just stole it. He told us when we got there, "What's the big deal of stealing? I've killed people."

Then I finally told his father about Eric's drug use, and we started the process together to get him help. The Veteran's Affairs in St. Louis is where we were directed for his treatment. It took a few months and lots of paperwork, but we got him into an outpatient program at John Cochran Hospital in St. Louis. It was a methadone treatment program for the drug addiction and counseling for his PTSD. I felt Eric wasn't in the right treatment, as he was surrounded by 50+ year-old veterans, not kids his age. And the doctors had so many patients. But he went and we prayed for the best, that this would cure him.

He wasn't allowed to drive while under treatment, so I drove him where he needed to go, most of the time. One morning he did drive, and I got the call that he'd been in an accident returning from the clinic. He had totaled my car on Troy-Scott Road. We were so blessed that no one was killed. The police officers were very kind when we told him he was a vet and being treated for PTSD.

We knew then that the methadone treatment hadn't worked. Not for Eric.

One day I was taking out the trash and heard something clinking in a Tide bottle. I opened it up and was sickened at the needles I saw. I knew then that his treatment hadn't cured him in the least. He was now using the needles he swore he didn't use. We realized that drugs had him like a vise, in their grip.

His father and I weren't good at the whole "tough love" thing, but that was a line that we couldn't tolerate. We told him he'd have to leave. I helped him find an apartment in Belleville. It was a pit, but what he could afford, and what you live in when you are a drug addict.

That is another of my regret points. Kicking him out. While he was in that apartment, he deteriorated. Physically, he had always worked out to the extreme – his body was that of a Marine long after he was one. But when he lived in that pit, he went way downhill. I didn't know it was a drug haven.

A few weeks after he moved there, a neighbor of Eric's that had my phone number (through some blessing of the Lord) called me and said, "You have to come and get your boy out or he is going to die." His father went alone. With body armor and his gun, he dragged him out of that pit. Eric went without a struggle. Now we knew it was time for more serious treatment, or we were going to lose him to heroin's death grip.

Around that same time, my mother's health was failing and she had moved in with us, too. Eric was always close with his grandmother and, even now, was a good caregiver for her. It was like he related to her in a different way - they were both challenged. He'd sit with her, talk with her, pray with her.

Eric, the boy who, at nine, wanted to be a priest. Right after being a Navy Seal, a priest was next on the list. He was a prayerful person, knew his bible and was a strong believer in God. That has always given me solace.

We struggled through the next months. It was July 4th, 2008 when I had one of those God moments. Those moments you plead with Him to give you guidance, understanding, strength. I was asking Him for guidance for Eric. Asking Him whether I should take Mom to an assisted living home. I pleaded, "Tell me what to do, God!"

Mom fell in the bathroom that afternoon. Eric was there with her and called the ambulance. Mom had broken her hip. She went to a nursing home, never to return to our home. She had no idea her compassionate caregiver was a drug addict.

Eric was put in treatment as part of his sentence for a previous overdose arrest. We found, again through the grace of God, a treatment program called ARCA (Assisted Recovery Centers of America). It turned out the people that ran it were in my church, people I knew but who had no idea that Eric was a drug addict.

Their program addressed holistically the mind, body and spirit, and it worked for him. It was expensive and private-pay only. I was grateful we could afford to have him in it, and I will always be grateful to them for their support of Eric and me and my family.

It was a program based on Naltrexone, a drug that keeps you from craving heroin and gets you through the withdrawals. Eric did well. He truly wanted to have his life back, to get well. It was a six-month program, which Eric was in from May through November 2008, and he did everything asked of him. He'd reached that point where his life was crap. He would cry, "I don't want to live like a junkie, in the gutter." He saw the pain in my face. He wanted desperately to be free from heroin's grip on him.

I know he didn't use then, because they tested him frequently. For those months, Eric was back to himself again. We were scared because his recovery was so tenuous, so fragile – we didn't quite trust him.

Eric's older brother had enlisted while Eric was in Iraq in 2004. He served a full year in Iraq and returned from his service in November, 2006. He and Eric eventually rented an apartment together. The family seemed to have returned to being fairly intact after these rough years, my prayers answered.

We went to a wedding in Dallas in the summer of 2008 and Eric got to enjoy time with his cousins and see all the family. Something he hadn't done for many years. We didn't trust him to stay home alone, not yet. And I have to say I was proud of him – he'd made it through this nightmare, and our Eric was back.

We enjoyed Thanksgiving as a family.

The next week it went bad.

On December 6th I was awakened at 3 a.m. by the phone ringing.

"Is this Laura?" "Yes." "This is Touchette Medical Center. I have one of your sons here. You need to come." Very matter-of-fact.

I could sense by her voice that it was to identify a body, not to see if he was ok.

Mary was sleeping, so one of us needed to stay. My husband said he would go. He went to the hospital and identified Eric's body. The nurse told him Eric was fighting, talking about fighting a war as he died. Eric had overdosed in a house in Cahokia with a combination of heroin and Xanax. We will never know just where or how or with whom he died. I believe he was with a Vietnam vet he met at the VA treatment center in St. Louis. Eric talked about him some, Jake, I think was his name. But we will never really know.

After those months of Eric being clean, I was caught off guard. If it had happened before his ARCA treatment, I was ready. Prepared, I was always expecting that call. Not this one. This didn't make sense. Couldn't be. I learned later about how addicts sometimes do a "self-selected test of personal control." Where they've been clean for many months and then use one more time, just to prove they are cured. But they use like they did before, way too much for their current sober body, and overdose because of this. Or maybe something happened to trigger his relapse, we will never know.

I couldn't view his body. I was grateful my husband and son had gone to identify him. I just couldn't bring myself to see him like that. Dead. I wanted to remember him as the beautiful boy he was. I have regret points there, too.

I went into full-shake mode. My body tremored. Just shook. If you've never experienced this, it's eerie. Like you aren't willing yourself to shake, aren't cold, but are trembling just the same.

But I was his mom. And now, I needed to let people know that he was dead. It was all just a numb blur, but I did it. I had to tell Mary, and his brother. And my family. I had to call work, too. My co-workers were so kind, so supportive.

We had arrangements to make. My heart was broken into pieces, my head was splitting apart and my body was shaking. My husband and I went to the funeral home. We'd never discussed Eric's wishes with him, but agreed to have him cremated. We think that was what he would have wanted. It was all just a slow-motion blur.

We decided to have the visitation at our church, St. Clare Catholic Church, in the hours before the funeral mass. So many people came – family, young people, church friends. I felt so supported by their presence. We asked TJ, his lifelong friend who had always stood by Eric, no matter how bad things got, to deliver the eulogy. And he did a moving remembrance honoring our son. He included a warning about drugs, which was just the right thing to do.

Overwhelmingly, people were kind. I think partly because he was a veteran suffering with PTSD and drug addiction. I allowed myself to block out any of the "mean" comments. I told it like it was: he died of a drug overdose.

Many, many relatives came. So many from other areas were visiting my mom in the nursing home, I had to go and tell her why they were in town. It broke my heart and hers.

The urn was buried in a full military funeral a few days later at Jefferson Barracks Cemetery in St. Louis. On that cold hill with the military salute ringing in my ears, I closed my eyes and could see the snowy winter day when my boy was born, just like it was yesterday."

———//———

Laura continued, solemnly sharing her grief journey.

———//———

"I go a couple of times a year to his grave site and just sit with my boy. Not really visit, just sit.

Eric's death took out my compass. My world was upside down, sideways, backwards, I couldn't figure out what was what. But I also had to function. I had Mary and she needed me, more than ever now. She threw herself right back into school and activities. That's how she coped with her grief.

It was God who stepped in and helped me function. My prayers were all for strength. To get out of bed. To make it through the day.

I have one good friend, Kathie, whom I'd confided in about Eric's issues all those years. Not many people knew, but she did. Every horrible detail. And she was there for me now, helping me get up in the morning and keep going. I thank God for her. And my brother and sister-in-law. They were there for me, they were my rocks.

I was blessed to be able to take six weeks off from work. I can't imagine how I would have functioned in the numb state I was in most of the time.

Our marriage wasn't close, but we hadn't had huge issues, either. Eric's death was to change that. At first, we supported each other, he had a bad day and I'd help him and he'd help me through a rough one.

Then, after a few months, my husband came to the realization that if he couldn't compartmentalize Eric's death, couldn't put it in a box and keep it there away from the rest of his life, he couldn't go on. He took a hard look at his life and didn't like what he saw. He wanted a change. And that change didn't include me. I was in denial that he'd leave. That we'd split, after all we'd been through.

But it happened. In 2010 he moved out and the divorce was final in 2013.

The death of a child changes a person. I think especially the traumatic way Eric died and the fact that we'd never know all the details. It shakes you to your core – takes you to your bones. Makes you question everything. And his answers lead him away from me, not towards me.

My mom also got worse, I think perhaps her heart was just broken about Eric's death, and she died in April of 2009.

Triple whammy. I was numb. My confidence was gone. Everything gone. The guilt was overwhelming.

My heart was broken. There was a hole I could visualize and feel, and I realized that I, too, had a choice to make. I could choose to quit, to hole up, or I could choose to try to fill it with love. To inch by inch fill it with love. I worked and prayed really hard to do that. Thank God for my family, they were my motivation to love, to go on.

I knew I needed help to get through this. I first found a Grief Support Group at Anderson Hospital. It was for all kinds of grief and was somewhat helpful. But I'm an introvert by nature and just wasn't very comfortable sharing my grief about Eric's drug addiction with those that had lost loved ones in more "normal" ways.

I started reading and praying, searching for answers to the Big W Question. Why? Why did You take Eric from us?

I started talking with my priest, and he led me to a loss support group, where I met the leader that had lost her daughter to drugs years earlier. She was very helpful and led me to a spiritual counselor who is my rock to this day, Sister Joan. She helped me to come to understand that suffering helps me to grow. She combined spiritual and practical advice to help me get back to living. It took me 4 to 5 years to work through it, but I am happy to say I did! I learned that I had to make the choice to let go of the "Why?" and live.

I found the Addiction Loss Support Group at Heartlinks Grief Center. That group is the one place where those around the table all understand what losing a child to drugs feels like. It is a safe, healing place, where I can feel "normal."

After years of struggle, I now have peace with the fact that Eric made choices. These were not my choices. Not my guilt. Eric was a smart, compassionate, gifted young man who touched many lives. I'll always remember him that way regardless of his choices.

I felt it was important to make some good come out of his death. A few weeks after Eric died, my husband and I were on a newscast, talking about his death. Ten years ago, PTSD was a fairly new term for an old condition, and the news reporter wanted to do a story on it and the link to drug addiction. I'm not sure that was the right thing for either of us, but we felt it was important to talk about PTSD, to talk about drug addiction, not hide it, to help others know where it could lead. The local papers ran stories, too.

What was taken away has helped me to grow. I had to put behind me the "regret points" – the things I wished I'd done differently, like signing his enlistment papers and not acknowledging his addiction and not getting him help quickly. I had to come to understand that God had a reason for it all.

Losing Eric brought me to another level of closeness with God, helped me to grow in my faith, because when you have that hole in your heart, faith is all that can fill it. I cling to this prayer:

"I thank you, Lord, for what you've given me
I thank you more for what you've taken away."

The word I'd use to describe this journey is "unexpected." And "life-altering." For those of you that think, "Drugs can't happen to my family," wake up! That's what I thought, too, and believe me, this nightmare can happen to any family. Watch for irrational behavior, sleep issues, mood changes and stealing. And fight, right away. Get them help, for you are fighting for their lives. There will always be bad people ready to sell your kids drugs. Watch them closely, and do all you can to strengthen your bonds as a nuclear family. Do all you can to make it harder for the grip of drugs to take hold of them.

What's hardest now, ten years after we lost Eric, is not the past, but the future. It's realizing that all of the hopes and dreams that I had for my beautiful soldier boy are gone, and it's not just my dreams, but the dreams of his brother and sister for him, also.

I take heart in that I am at peace that Eric is OK now. I've heard his voice and know he's still being compassionate. A few years after his death, when the tragic shooting occurred in New Town at Sandy Hook Elementary School on December 14, 2012, I was at work. We were all upset, but went about our day – seeing people in the lab, working in the blood bank. When I got home, "The Cry" came upon me. That cry that comes from deep within, the cry of despair for loss, the cry of a mother who has lost a child, and knows what's ahead for those parents. I was standing at my kitchen sink lost in The Cry and I heard Eric's voice, "Momma (he always called me that), "Momma, it's okay. I've got Benjamin."

I didn't know what to think about this until a few days later when they released the names of the dead children. Benjamin Wheeler. Age 6. Eric's got him."

Note to the reader: The correspondence between the father of Benjamin Wheeler and I, expressing his gratitude for asking permission to use Benjamin's name in this story, can be found in Appendix G.

Lyrics to "Things Won't Ever Be the Same"
Performed by 50/50:

> I'll just ignore you or walk away
> Try another day, may take the same
> There's a point you can't see
> It's deep inside, all over me
> If I forgive you, will you let me choose
> Choose between my love and you
>
> Things won't ever be the same
> Another day is past
> Another memory won't last
> Just thrown away my dreams
> I gave it all for you
> Whatever happens
> It doesn't matter anyway
>
> Cause things won't ever be the same. The same.

Things Won't Ever Be the Same
– Grief Reflections –
By Diana Cuddeback, LCSW

Each story in this book allows the reader a glimpse into the lives and hearts of the storyteller. Laura is brave and gracious in the honest remembrance she shares. Laura's insightful picture of her son, Eric, and their experience of PTSD and addiction holds lessons for those still battling addiction, and for those grieving addiction losses.

Laura beautifully illustrates a key component of grief with this statement: "**I lost my compass.**" She goes on to explain that losing her compass impacted her ability to manage basic life. Grief impacts people mentally, emotionally, physically, psychologically, and socially. What you knew to be true and predictable is often lost. People explain that they feel numb and dislocated, like they don't know where they belong or what they are meant to do next. Laura says it best, "My world was upside down, sideways, backwards; I couldn't figure out what was what."

To manage this compass loss and the additional changes which losing Eric had brought to her life, Laura found a True North heading in caring for her daughter who was still at home. Mary needed her mother. **Finding a *have-to* focus** can give you a direction to move towards when your compass is broken by grief. Laura suggests you **lean in to faith, prayer and spiritual practice** as well. She found consolation in specific prayers and practices.

This consolation is something only an individual griever can find. No one can do it for him or her. If you are supporting a grieving person, go ahead and share ideas, sayings, memes, prayers, and books. Be open to receiving no comment on them at all. Or be ready to hear either negative or positive feedback. Understand that for any of these things to be useful, it must have individual meaning to the grieving person. It has to make sense to him or her. It must provide consolation. Making and finding meaning cannot come from you, so don't push your interpretation. What seems powerful to you, or your faith perspective, may fall flat for the person you are trying to support.

Laura discusses how the grief experience makes you "question everything," and "shakes you to your bones." There are no magic answers and no magic words for someone shaken to their bones. Be quiet. Just **be present and create safety,** like the people that Laura mentions. It may not seem like much, but it can be everything.

Laura teaches us several other important things. Grief brings change. **Allow yourself to be changed**, to live differently. Don't spend your energy fighting change. Laura also **actively acknowledges and seeks to manage her regrets and "should-haves."** She is aware of them and works on them. She forgives herself and the people around her. Laura doesn't waste energy on bitterness. Instead, she has sought support in groups and through spiritual counseling. **Seek support,** including professional support.

Laura, who is a very private person, has also chosen to **share openly to inform others,** through an early interview with the local newspaper and by helping with group facilitation. All of these things have helped Laura to reorient her personal compass and continue working to find a True North to guide her through grief. Grief is a lifetime process, not a project to finish. Stay open to the options and allow change.

Author Megan Devine has so beautifully said, "Some things in life cannot be fixed. They can only be carried." Finding ways to help you carry the grief and care for your internal compass is an important focus.

CHAPTER NINE

Devastated – The Story That Cannot Yet Be Told

By Ellen Krohne

Dear readers, there is one more family's story that was written for this book. After it was finished, the family just couldn't bear it, and they asked me not to include the story of their family's addiction journey. The remaining children felt devastated all over again by its telling. It was too painful, too fresh, too much still happening in real time.

The story is about a family that dealt with drug addiction for decades. The father had chronic hip pain, and was prescribed opioids that led to years of heroin addiction when his prescriptions were cut off. Two of the family's four children also became addicts. One very recently lost her life to a heroin overdose.

Another child is once again in counseling and rehab, working hard to beat her addiction. The father finally went to rehab and is clean now, but his recovery is tenuous.

The mother in this family is so brave, so strong, and so heart-broken. She's a self-described "fixer." Trying for years and years to cure them and, as she admits, perhaps she enabled them. She graciously offers the following guidance, gained from the years of dealing with her own personal nightmare:

"I look back, and see how naïve I was about drugs. Even after my husband's addiction and all our problems, I never dreamt that my children were using, even when the signs were all there.

I look back and see that I may have enabled their addiction. I'd pray and yell and cry and beg, but I'd give them money and let them stay with me. I know now there must be professional intervention, medical intervention, to successfully rehabilitate a drug user. And they have to be ready, and want to be clean.

As parents, we think we need to protect our children. It's like when a little child touches a hot stove, they learn not to do that again. With drug addicts, you think you can save and protect them, but they have to learn that there are consequences – jail, homelessness, even death. We have to let them touch the stove to learn, before it's too late."

Part III

The Opioid Crisis – Conclusions

————— // —————

In Chapter Ten, Matthew Ellis outlines the specifics we have learned from the families' stories about the opioid crisis, the role that stigma plays in this crisis, and identifies actions we can each take toward making a difference in helping the opioid crisis to end. He describes both policy change imperatives and changes to current treatment options.

In Chapter Eleven, I describe education and prevention strategies that are currently being employed, and provide resources and suggestions for what each of us can do to prevent a loved one, particularly a child, from starting down the path of substance use.

Chapter Twelve includes closing thoughts from Diana and, finally, from me.

CHAPTER TEN

The Road Ahead for Fighting Addictions: Removing Stigma and Other Obstacles

By Matthew Ellis, MPE

The Butterfly Effect is a theory which suggests that small changes have the potential to cause significant, even catastrophic, effects down the road, like the flapping of a butterfly's wings on one side of the world somehow resulting in a tsunami in the other. Life is a never-ending series of minor and major events, products of circumstances that create an experience unique to each person, to each society. Despite humanity's best efforts, we cannot predict the future. We cannot predict how the interactions of hundreds of thousands of variables will appear, disappear, or interact throughout one's existence.

Our society's cultural, legal, legislative, and economic norms have all intertwined with the dynamic forces of opioid supply and demand, resulting in an opioid epidemic and the loss of hundreds of thousands of lives. Likewise, the stories and lives of the parents and children described in the previous chapters will never be repeated by anyone else; they are deeply personal, emotional and individual. They are products of a multitude of contexts, among them social, cultural, interpersonal and individual. So how do we as a society learn from the unique experiences of others?

In the introduction, I noted that the opioid epidemic is a contradiction of sorts, a unique drug epidemic that still bears similarities to the prior ones. The same can be said of this collection of stories. Each story belongs to that individual person and will never exist for anyone else. And yet, these stories have similarities - themes and experiences that bear resemblance to one another – from which we can take lessons in order to grow, both as individuals and as a society. They are speaking. Let us listen.

———— // ————

Much of what we can learn from these experiences is rooted in a dynamic, pervasive, and yet misunderstood concept: stigma. Stigma can be difficult to define, but one of the more common definitions stems from sociology and focuses on labeling the individual. The label which refers to this topic is often the label of "addict." Labeling can lead to "stereotyping, separation, emotional reactions, status loss and discrimination, which can only occur in the presence of a power differential between those labelled and those who label.[1]" Put another way, it is a "set of negative attitudes and beliefs that motivate individuals to fear, reject, avoid and discriminate against people[2]."

When we look at the myriad of factors involved in the opioid epidemic, stigma, while not overtly apparent, is manifested in a variety of ways and came, sometimes surprisingly, from a diverse group of individuals and professions. The prevalence of stigma is hard to quantify, but it is readily apparent in the experiences described in this book. These instances serve as examples of the role stigma plays in the following areas, each of which is detailed in the sections below:

- Understanding the Nature of Addiction
- The Treatment Gap
- Mental Health and Addiction
- In the Capitol
- The De-stigmatization of Heroin

It is important for us to understand why and how the opioid epidemic occurred, in order to prevent another such event from occurring again. While there are a number of obvious factors involved, such as the liberal use of opioid prescriptions, it is the not-so-obvious factors that must also be understood and addressed, although that is not always easy. The notion of stigma raises questions of personal beliefs, societal perceptions, and moral values. These can potentially lead to emotional discussions, even more so when individuals have lost a loved one, been victimized, or had negative experiences with those suffering from addiction. This conclusion should serve as a stepping stone to constructive conversations about the nature of addiction, its root causes, and where we can better serve not only those who need our help, but society overall.

Understanding the Nature of Addiction

The United States has a history of defining addiction as an individual choice that is inherently immoral and we, as a society, have assumed the right to judge those who have "chosen" to be an addict. For centuries, those who indulged in excess were judged, and excessive use was seen as a moral failing of the individual. In the 1970's, drug policies centered on punishment and prohibition, and so those who used drugs were seen as criminals who made a personal choice to break the law. This concept of addiction flourished and, in conjunction with criminal behavior and drug use among inner-city and minority communities being sensationalized in the media, created a cultural norm of viewing addicts as people who made a choice to engage in criminal behavior. Indeed, vestiges of these negative judgments of addicts were evident throughout these stories, even in a professional setting or from those inside the social networks of the families:

- *Scum of the earth* – nurse assisting in Ryan's medical care
- *The only people that deserve to die are drug addicts* – associate of Ryan's family
- *Put all those drug dealers and addicts in jail* – family member of Alaina
- *The police were at the hospital too, and they were just plain rude. "This happens every day"* – Michael's father
- *I allowed myself to block out any of the "mean" comments* – Eric's mother

Using the moral theory of addiction, individuals should be able to choose to stop using drugs, just like they chose to start using them. This, also, is a pervasive viewpoint that was reflected in these stories:

- *He [Alaina's father] just could not understand why she couldn't do the same [quit cold turkey].* – Alaina's mother

– Why did he do drugs, why didn't he just quit? – work associate of Ryan's family member

In the 1980's, the disease model was popularized, viewing addiction as a biological disease that could be treated like other medical diagnoses. In this model, people began to understand that addiction is something that happens in the brain, and overcoming it requires medical treatment. However, for many the decision to initiate drug use was still an individual choice that carried moral connotations. As noted:

– My kid would never do that – associate of Ryan's family member

– Your child made a choice to be addicted. I knew in my heart that's what they thought. – Alaina's mother

– Your grief is different than if Alaina had died of cancer, because she made a choice. – family member of Alaina

– I believe some people think less of him and me for dying this way – Michaels' father

During this same time period, as addiction was being viewed as a disease, a parallel movement arose that viewed co-dependency as a symptom of the disease, essentially saying that friends and family who provided empathy, social support and care to addicts were enabling the addiction. The co-dependency movement popularized "tough love" and pushing addicts to hit "rock bottom." "Tough love" makes sense when considered in context with addiction as a choice; a family sets limits in the hopes that this will force an individual to choose to stop being an addict. While it can cause great pain to those families involved, for some this approach has worked. It also is understandable when a family feels that they have run out of options. Addiction affects not only the user, but those closest to him/her as well, and the frustrations, fear and pain that occur over and over again take a toll on those involved, leading to feelings of being lost or not knowing what to do. "Tough love" feels like the last stop of a complicated journey.

However, "tough love" also removes love and support from an individual who likely already experiences negative feelings, for which drug use acts as a coping mechanism. "Tough love" can end up amplifying those negative feelings and the feelings of loneliness, fear or anger. The result can be the opposite of what was intended: increasing drug use or engaging in behaviors that can lead to worse outcomes.

While the stories in Part Two often mention the decision to either engage in or refrain from tough love, a difficult decision for any family found in such dire situations, the evidence from research shows two key points of note. First, providing empathy and social support have been shown to have a greater positive impact on recovery than "tough love." And second, allowing someone to hit "rock bottom" can result in worse outcomes, possibly even death, as "rock bottom" may mean an overdose from which one cannot recover[3, 4].

Currently, a new model is gaining traction: understanding addiction as a learning disorder[4]. While there are biological undertones, it is not enough to merely provide a drug like buprenorphine (e.g., Suboxone, Subutex) to prevent withdrawals and reduce cravings. Drug use, like a habit, must be "unlearned." What lends credence to this argument is the fact that most individuals with an addiction, including those mentioned here, relapse regardless of the treatment or how well they may be recovering. Ryan, Eric and Johnny were considered by their families to be doing well, and their deaths from overdose came as a surprise.

Research and qualitative data have shown that the majority of users, by the time they enter treatment, are no longer using drugs to get high[5]. They primarily use either to stave off withdrawal sickness, or because they feel they cannot stop. The words of those lost are the most impactful here:

– *It wasn't my choice, it's not what I want.* – Ryan

– *I don't want to live like a junkie, in the gutter* – Eric

– *I just can't get off the crack. Can't stop this.* – Melody

In the context of a learned behavior, it may be understood that we may need to replace current treatment practices with more substantial, long-term care that includes mental health, and social services may be needed in order to "unlearn" drug behaviors.

Regardless of which addiction model one prefers, it should be agreed that one of the primary ways of interrupting addiction is through effective substance use treatment. However, an important component of the cycle of addiction, including relapse (and thus, negative outcomes that lead to "rock bottom" or "tough love") is the lack of accessibility and availability of substance use treatment for a majority of opioid users.

The Treatment Gap

Recent estimates have suggested that just 10-20% of those with opioid use disorder receive treatment[6]. For adolescents, this number is even lower[7]. This treatment gap highlights one of the primary issues in combating the opioid epidemic: inaccessible or inadequate treatment[6-14]. This was evident in many of the preceding stories.

Ryan had to travel to Florida and Chicago. Alaina had to go to Quincy, IL, was refused locally because of a lack of insurance, and then had to travel again to Decatur, Ill. Johnny was sent to Central Illinois but was kicked out due to lack of insurance. The methadone treatment at the VA wasn't working for Eric. Melody couldn't find a local treatment center because she had no insurance, but then as her mother described:

> When we got to the rehab in Springfield, Melody begged them to let her in. But their story had changed and they didn't have a bed for her then, so they put her on the waiting list. They said by mid-November they would have a bed.

Although the expansion of treatment is a primary goal of the current government administration, there continue to be many barriers to the provision of treatment, which primarily center on medication-assisted treatments (MAT) methadone and buprenorphine (e.g., Suboxone, Subutex.)

Methadone, for many years, was the most commonly used MAT. It is an opioid that is used to wean those addicted to other opioids by preventing withdrawal symptoms and cravings. Methadone is only available at methadone maintenance clinics, and has been shown to be an effective treatment for opioid use disorder. However, expansion of these clinics is also often roadblocked on a community level, particularly for the medication-assisted treatment, methadone. Efforts to open more methadone clinics are often met with opposition in the communities they service, a mentality commonly referred to as NIMBY (Not In My Back Yard.) Treatment centers, in the minds of many in the community, are often associated with criminality or bringing in undesirables, even if that community is already being ravaged by substance use. Local opposition often prevents the opening of new clinics, creating wide gaps in service delivery.

Buprenorphine is a newer form of MAT that works in a similar fashion to methadone, but has become a more common form of treatment due to its ability to be prescribed in office-based medical settings after the doctor has received a waiver to do so. However, only 5% of the nation's doctors have obtained the waiver that allows them to prescribe buprenorphine. And for those who do prescribe it, many do not come close to the maximum limit to which they are allowed to prescribe, which has recently been increased from 100 to 275. Studies have shown that this is because many physicians hold negative stigma towards those with addiction, not wanting to deal with the "hassle" of treating substance users, particularly those without insurance. For many areas, particularly rural areas, the few treatment facilities or doctors which are available are often at capacity and cannot take in new patients, even if they want to do so. And when a space does become available, funding for treatment, as noted in several stories, becomes a primary issue for acceptance or denial of care.

Complicating the picture of treatment is funding and coverage. Questions remain on who should fund treatment, to what degree it should be covered by insurance, what forms should be covered by insurance (e.g., is it MAT only, or will counseling be included?), what forms should be available to an individual (e.g., detox, inpatient, outpatient, etc.), whether Medicaid expansion should help, and to what degree the government should play a role. While expansion of treatment was a hallmark of the recent opioid spending package, it is unclear whether it will be enough, or how it will be spent by those who receive such funds.

In addition, medication-assisted methods treat opioid addiction at a biological level. This ignores two crucial factors that are often disregarded, both in prevention and in treatment strategies for addiction: other substance use, and mental health, the latter of which will be discussed in the next section of this chapter.

The vast majority of addicts are polysubstance users, meaning they use more than just one type of drug[15-24]. For instance, co-occurring use of opioids and methamphetamine (e.g., meth, chalk, ice, and crystal) are drastically increasing. Prescription opioids are often used with anti-anxiety medication such as Xanax and Valium, and both of these are often used with alcohol. Not only does this increase the risk of adverse events, particularly overdoses, but it highlights the fact that treatment cannot be limited to a single drug alone. Buprenorphine and methadone alone can do nothing to address the wide variety of other drugs available and used by those with addiction.

The use of multiple substances also underscores one of the other key factors of addiction and treatment: mental health.

Mental Health and Addiction

As noted in the introduction, mental health plays a prominent and important role in the development of addiction and persistent drug use. Indeed, in 1985, Edward Khantzian published a theory of substance use disorders centered around the "self-medication" of mental health issues. Such issues include stressors from daily life, marked life events, diagnosed mental disorders, and sub-clinical diagnoses like depression and anxiety that exist, but maybe not to a degree that meets the criteria for medical treatment. While at the time this was minimized in favor of the moral or disease models of addiction, the wealth of data supporting the link between mental health and addiction have brought this theory back into the spotlight. While these relationships were not explicitly linked in the preceding stories, these individuals experienced stressful life events (e.g., Ryan's girlfriend and Alaina's father were diagnosed with cancer; Eric and Alaina both lost grandparents with whom they were close), mental health issues (e.g., Alaina had underlying depression and anxiety, and Eric was diagnosed with Post-Traumatic Stress Disorder) and trauma (e.g., Melody was sexually assaulted).

Unfortunately, here we may be coming to the heart of the reason that addiction has been such a challenge in the United States: both mental health AND addiction are stigmatized in our society, and yet are intimately linked[25-27]. And it is nearly impossible to get adequate treatment for both at the same time. Stigma is not limited to addiction. In the United States, there is significant stigma attached to admitting that one has mental health problems, or is seeking help for mental health issues.

Despite the fact that mental health problems are the leading cause of disability in the United States[28], over half (57.4%) of those with mental illness do not receive any services. Much of this is tied to society's perception of mental health. Only 7% of Americans feel that mental illness can be overcome[29]. Despite our increased understanding of mental health and illness, the perception that mentally ill individuals are dangerous has actually *increased* over time[30]. Just a quarter of those with mental illness feel that others are caring or sympathetic to them[31]. And health professionals, even mental health professionals, often hold negative attitudes towards the mentally ill, just as they do towards addiction[32-34].

This leads those suffering from mental health issues to avoid seeking help, reducing their potential for recovery. If they do seek help it is, on average, *eight to ten years* after the initial onset of symptoms[35]. The stigma of mental illness has been shown to be associated with increased social isolation, loneliness, impairment in social networks, reduced social capital, and reduced community participation. For adults, it is linked with discrimination in housing, education, employment, the criminal justice system, and health and social care. For adolescents, stigma has been associated with academic underachievement, juvenile delinquency, unemployment, crime, substance use, and anti-social behavior. Suicide, often linked with mental illness, is the leading cause of death among adolescents[2, 25-28, 31, 36-39].

All of the issues noted above can predicate or exacerbate substance use. On an individual level, someone with mental health issues, or someone struggling to cope with significant stress, may feel pressured by cultural norms to deal with these issues on their own, rather than seek help. They may feel that seeking treatment means that something is wrong with them, or they are flawed, and instead seek to merely numb themselves or escape from their life through other means such as drugs. If problematic drug use develops, they may then refuse to admit they have an addiction, due to the negative stigma associated with addiction. They may fear a loss of social support or, more importantly, may delay or refuse altogether to seek treatment until use has progressed to a more extreme point, or until more adverse outcomes have occurred.

Rates of mental illness among substance users are significantly higher than in the general population. According to the National Institute of Drug Abuse, about half of substance users will also experience a co-occurring mental illness[40, 41]. Mental illness has been shown to be a risk factor for opioid use disorder, yet substance use can also precede mental illness, or make existing issues worse. Opioids can serve as a coping mechanism, or their use can lead to behaviors or decisions that lead to negative outcomes, which can also impact mental health. For many individuals, the two are inextricably linked.

We must recognize that addiction is not just about drug use, but involves an array of other forces, both internal and external. Currently, though, efforts are being made to test, with promising results, the utility of a "continuum of care," as has been standardized for HIV treatment. The continuum of care for HIV treatment involves wrap-around services that promote treatment and services across multiple domains. They involve a staged regimen that reflects the understanding that providing appropriate treatment and care is a long-term process that involves more than just the administration of a treatment drug. For opioid addiction, this would include not only medication-assisted treatment, but mental health services and social services over a significant period of time, in order to move oneself out of addiction, and essentially treat the disease rather than the symptoms.

In the Capitol

The preceding stories and quotes may seem to imply that these thoughts and beliefs regarding addiction are individualized and, while painful for the families involved, do little to no lasting harm to society as a whole. The reality, though, is that stigma has infiltrated nearly every aspect of how addiction is treated and managed in the United States.

Stigma has been shown to have a negative and significant impact on local, state and federal policies. It has been associated with decreased support for policies to mitigate mental illness and substance use disorder. In 2016, in the midst of the opioid epidemic, less than half of Americans were willing to increase spending on mental illness (47%) or substance use disorders (39%)[27]. Those with negative associations with mental health or substance use disorder had decreased support for improving insurance benefits for both conditions, and increased support for punitive measures[27].

This is most readily apparent as we see American public opposition to the harm-reduction strategies that have been approved in many other Western nations. These are common-sense practices which have been shown by many scientific studies to reduce the negative health outcomes of opioid use, such as disease transmission and overdose deaths.

On a legislative level, bills allowing safe-injection facilities, where users can inject under the supervision of a medical professional, needle exchanges that provide clean needles to prevent disease transmission (e.g., HIV), and test strips that can identify the deadly narcotic fentanyl in one's heroin, are almost never passed. In fact, in some states these were explicitly made illegal. Despite research studies suggesting these harm-reduction strategies save lives and reduce outcomes like disease transmission [42-45], policymakers repeatedly put forth the belief that these harm-reduction strategies only encourage more drug use, using this mistaken belief as a rationale for not saving lives.

Even prescription drug monitoring programs (PDMP), designed to prevent doctor shopping for opioids and to encourage more careful prescription practices by physicians, have been the subject of debate. A politician in Missouri, the only state without a PDMP, blocked legislation to implement a PDMP and commented about those with addictions, "If they overdose and kill themselves, it just removes them from the gene pool.[46]"

These stories show the realities of the current situation, and demonstrate why the opposite mentality is important.

> *"She did what she had to, to get the drugs. And, I did what I had to, to keep her alive...I'd give her $20.00 to buy gas or cigarettes, knowing she was getting her drugs, but also knowing she wouldn't be giving some guy a blow job for them."*
> – Alaina's mother

> *"I did what I had to, to help keep her alive. Some days I drove her to her dealer to get her crack. Sometimes in the middle of the night...you do what you have to, to keep your kid alive."* – Melody's mother

Policies should respond to the debilitating nature of addiction, and provide ways to mitigate its worst outcomes. One of the positive outcomes of recent note is the increased distribution of naloxone beyond just first responders. Access to the drug is now being provided to anyone who wants it, with some state or community programs even subsidizing the costs in order to get it in the hands of users and their families. Bystander naloxone administration, in conjunction with overdose education programs and kit distribution, has shown to be effective in increasing the odds of recovery within studied communities. Ryan, Alaina and Eric's stories all indicate a prior history of overdoses that did not result in death. Ryan, John, Michael and Eric succumbed to overdose. Things may have been different if they had had a safe space to inject, and could have tested their drug for fentanyl, or had naloxone nearby.

The De-stigmatization of Heroin

Michael's story is unique among the others. His family did not go through the ups and downs of addiction and recovery. They did not have to hide their wallets or search for a rehab clinic. It is plausible that his overdose was the product of a singular instance of recreational use gone wrong. For some, this fact will make Michael's the most difficult story from which to learn. They may be less likely to question what anyone could have done to prevent this from happening to Michael. However, Michael's story teaches us one final, and crucially important, lesson about stigma: sometimes stigma is useful.

Throughout these stories, there was a stigma against heroin use, both among the families and among those with the addiction.

I was scared of heroin, that was for junkies – Johnny's father

Melody did those pills, but I knew she'd never do heroin – Melody's mother

In the waiting room, she met two guys…she asked "what are you in for?" When they answered 'Heroin', she wouldn't stay. She didn't want anything to do with heroin, even in the facility that could save her. – Melody's mother

He was now using the needles he swore he wouldn't use – Eric's mother

As noted in Chapter One, heroin became cheaper and easier to find, and so its popularity and use has increased as suppliers have flooded the market. This has had the effect of increasing the use of heroin as a recreational drug, and not just a drug for advanced users. A secondary effect has been the normalization of heroin, reducing its stigma, primarily for younger individuals who are either experimenting with it, taking it as a party drug, or initiating their opioid use with it, rather than travelling the previously common pathway of starting with prescription opioids and graduating to heroin.

Michael's story illustrates the danger of this changing stigma. It is difficult for any user, let alone an inexperienced one, to know what the purity of their heroin is, what other drugs are mixed in with it, how much to take at one time, or what their tolerance to it will be. All of these unknowns increase the likelihood of a fatal overdose, even if the drug is taken just once.

We must understand that heroin is not a drug just of "junkies" or advanced users, but exists as a real possibility for anyone to use, particularly young adults who are experimenting. Naloxone needs to be more widely distributed as a precautionary measure. And fentanyl test strips need to be available for anyone who wishes to avoid the deadly combination of fentanyl and heroin.

Prevention and education programs need to focus more on heroin, and not just on prescription opioids. In some ways, increasing the stigma could be useful here as a protective factor. The changing norms of cigarette smoking, particularly among teenagers, over the last few decades are a good example of this. Prevention and education efforts have shifted the social perception of cigarette smoking to be increasingly negative, leading current smoking rates to drop to their lowest point.

What Can We Do?

The question that is often asked is, "What can we do?" First, our society must understand that addiction exists and can exist for *anyone*. Recognizing stigma, whether inherent in yourself or in others, is an important first step. It should be noted here that a bias or stigma is a part of everyone, and we should not be ashamed to admit it. In order to grow, we must recognize and respond to these inherent traits, not ignore or pretend we are above them. This is the larger purpose of this book.

Understanding, empathy and support derive from hearing the experiences of others. Research supports this storytelling as one of the key ways of overcoming stigma. In your community, creating spaces for addicts or their families to speak about these issues openly and honestly can go a long way in shaping your community's reaction to the opioid epidemic. This could lead to greater support for interventions, such as the opening of a methadone clinic in your community, or may lead a local physician to begin prescribing buprenorphine.

Gaining knowledge and understanding the structural barriers have also been associated with decreased stigma, and with increased support for policies that improve treatment for substance use disorders and mental illness. In that regard, we hope that both Chapter One and this chapter will provide you with a more informed perspective of the opioid epidemic. We encourage you to seek out other sources of information as well.

For substance use treatment to be most effective, mental health must be a core component. This will allow treatment of the underlying issues - the disease, and not just the symptoms. To bolster the prevention of substance use in general, we need a greater emphasis on individual mental health care, education on healthy coping skills, empathy through social support, and acceptance that mental health issues are universal and must not be stigmatized. The National Institute of Mental Health's "Let's Talk

About It" campaign focuses on four components that are meant to not only decrease stigma for mental health and substance use, but can also serve as tenets for those families who may feel lost in someone's cycle of addiction or mental illness: Don't be afraid to talk; Be supportive; Encourage treatment; and Speak positively.

On a more practical level, attending overdose education programs and being willing to engage in bystander naloxone administration can also serve as a way to take action. Setting up an education program, working with others to distribute naloxone into the community (e.g., known users or families/friends of known users) or simply encouraging those in the community with no experience with addiction to attend or to carry naloxone.

Finally, harm-reduction strategies save lives. Advocacy based on the stories and experiences of those who have suffered are our greatest tools in fighting the stigmatized views of addiction. While many are no longer with us, their lives should serve to help others in need, to prevent other families from suffering like those here, who bravely shared their experiences so that we, as individuals and as a society, can grow. While it is difficult to treat and manage addiction, we can take steps to at least provide safe pathways of use that can limit the loss of life. Needle exchanges, safe testing facilities, and fentanyl test strips save lives, and we should be advocating for these interventions.

For anyone concerned about this issue, becoming active in social justice groups, lobbying for or against legislation, and meeting face-to-face with politicians, educators and organizations that have a direct impact on prevention and treatment strategies, are all ways to fight back against stigma. In your everyday relationships with others, speaking up when you hear expressions of stigma about mental health or substance use disorders can create a snowball effect, where your social network may become better educated about these issues, and can then distribute that knowledge through other social networks.

Reducing stigma is an issue that needs to be tackled across multiple levels in order for change to occur. This book is a step in that direction, with more effort needed to provide safe spaces for both individuals suffering from addiction and their loved ones, to be able to share their stories, and to have others share their stories. It is these stories that have the greatest impact. Be willing to listen, to speak, to share and to change, in order to create that Butterfly Effect of positive change in America.

Endnotes

1. Link, B.G., et al., *Measuring mental illness stigma.* Schizophr Bull, 2004. **30**(3): p. 511-41.

2. Parcesepe, A.M. and L.J. Cabassa, *Public stigma of mental illness in the United States: a systematic literature review.* Adm Policy Ment Health, 2013. **40**(5): p. 384-99.

3. White, W., Miller, W., *The use of confrontation in addiction treatment: History, science and time for change.* Counselor, 2007. 8(4): p. 12-30.

4. Salavitz, M., *Unbroken Brain: A Revolutionary New Way of Understanding Addiction.* 2016, New York City, NY: Picador St. Martin's Press.

5. Cicero, T.J. and M.S. Ellis, *The prescription opioid epidemic: a review of qualitative studies on the progression from initial use to abuse.* Dialogues Clin Neurosci, 2017. **19**(3): p. 259-269.

6. Saloner, B. and S. Karthikeyan, *Changes in Substance Abuse Treatment Use Among Individuals With Opioid Use Disorders in the United States, 2004-2013.* JAMA, 2015. **314**(14): p. 1515-7.

7. Feder, K.A., N. Krawczyk, and B. Saloner, *Medication-Assisted Treatment for Adolescents in Specialty Treatment for Opioid Use Disorder.* J Adolesc Health, 2017. **60**(6): p. 747-750.

8. Volkow, N.D., et al., *Medication-assisted therapies--tackling the opioid-overdose epidemic.* N Engl J Med, 2014. **370**(22): p. 2063-6.

9. Jones, C.M., et al., *National and State Treatment Need and Capacity for Opioid Agonist Medication-Assisted Treatment.* Am J Public Health, 2015. **105**(8): p. e55-63.

10. Mark, T.L., et al., *Medicaid coverage of medications to treat alcohol and opioid dependence.* J Subst Abuse Treat, 2015. **55**: p. 1-5.

11. Burns, R.M., et al., *Policies related to opioid agonist therapy for opioid use disorders: The evolution of state policies from 2004 to 2013.* Subst Abus, 2016. **37**(1): p. 63-9.

12. Stein, B.D., et al., *Supply of buprenorphine waivered physicians: the influence of state policies.* J Subst Abuse Treat, 2015. **48**(1): p. 104-11.

13. Huhn, A.S. and K.E. Dunn, *Why aren't physicians prescribing more buprenorphine?* J Subst Abuse Treat, 2017. **78**: p. 1-7.

14. Kermack, A., et al., *Buprenorphine prescribing practice trends and attitudes among New York providers.* J Subst Abuse Treat, 2017. **74**: p. 1-6.

15. Cicero, T.J., M.S. Ellis, and Z.A. Kasper, *Psychoactive substance use prior to the development of iatrogenic opioid abuse: A descriptive analysis of treatment-seeking opioid abusers.* Addict Behav, 2017. **65**: p. 242-244.

16. Connor, J.P., et al., *Polysubstance use in cannabis users referred for treatment: drug use profiles, psychiatric comorbidity and cannabis-related beliefs.* Front Psychiatry, 2013. **4**: p. 79.

17. Connor, J.P., et al., *Polysubstance use: diagnostic challenges, patterns of use and health.* Curr Opin Psychiatry, 2014. **27**(4): p. 269-75.

18. Jarlenski, M., et al., *Polysubstance Use Among US Women of Reproductive Age Who Use Opioids for Nonmedical Reasons.* Am J Public Health, 2017. **107**(8): p. 1308-1310.

19. Timko, C., et al., *Polysubstance Use by Stimulant Users: Health Outcomes Over Three Years.* J Stud Alcohol Drugs, 2018. **79**(5): p. 799-807.

20. Timko, C., et al., *Polysubstance use by psychiatry inpatients with co-occurring mental health and substance use disorders.* Drug Alcohol Depend, 2017. **180**: p. 319-322.

21. Al-Tayyib, A., et al., *Heroin and Methamphetamine Injection: An Emerging Drug Use Pattern.* Subst Use Misuse, 2017. **52**(8): p. 1051-1058.

22. Ellis, M.S., Z.A. Kasper, and T.J. Cicero, *Twin epidemics: The surging rise of methamphetamine use in chronic opioid users.* Drug Alcohol Depend, 2018. **193**: p. 14-20.

23. Hedegaard, H., et al., *Drugs Most Frequently Involved in Drug Overdose Deaths: United States, 2011-2016.* Natl Vital Stat Rep, 2018. **67**(9): p. 1-14.

24. Sun, E.C., et al., *Association between concurrent use of prescription opioids and benzodiazepines and overdose: retrospective analysis.* BMJ, 2017. **356**: p. j760.

25. Barry, C.L., et al., *Stigma, discrimination, treatment effectiveness, and policy: public views about drug addiction and mental illness.* Psychiatr Serv, 2014. **65**(10): p. 1269-72.

26. Kennedy-Hendricks, A., et al., *Social Stigma Toward Persons With Prescription Opioid Use Disorder: Associations With Public Support for Punitive and Public Health-Oriented Policies.* Psychiatr Serv, 2017. **68**(5): p. 462-469.

27. McGinty, E., et al., *Communication Strategies to Counter Stigma and Improve Mental Illness and Substance Use Disorder Policy.* Psychiatr Serv, 2018. **69**(2): p. 136-146.

28. Wong, E.C., et al., *Differential Association of Stigma with Perceived Need and Mental Health Service Use.* J Nerv Ment Dis, 2018. **206**(6): p. 461-468.

29. Seeman, N., et al., *World survey of mental illness stigma.* J Affect Disord, 2016. **190**: p. 115-121.

30. Phelan, J., Link, BG, Stueve, A, Pescosolido, BA, *Public Conceptions of Mental Illness in 1950 and 1996: What Is Mental Illness andIs It to be Feared?* J Health Soc Behav, 2000. **41**(2): p. 188-207.

31. Centers for Disease Control and Prevention, S.A.a.M.H.S.A., N.I.o. National Association of County Behavioral Health & Developmental Disability Directors, and T.C.C.M.H.P. Mental Health, *Attitudes Toward Mental Illness: Results from the Behavioral Risk Factor Surveillance System.* Atlanta (GA); , 2012. **Centers for Disease Control and Prevention**.

32. Dockery, L., et al., *Stigma- and non-stigma-related treatment barriers to mental healthcare reported by service users and caregivers.* Psychiatry Res, 2015. **228**(3): p. 612-9.

33. van Boekel, L.C., et al., *Stigma among health professionals towards patients with substance use disorders and its consequences for healthcare delivery: systematic review.* Drug Alcohol Depend, 2013. **131**(1-2): p. 23-35.

34. Knaak, S., E. Mantler, and A. Szeto, *Mental illness-related stigma in healthcare: Barriers to access and care and evidence-based solutions.* Healthc Manage Forum, 2017. **30**(2): p. 111-116.

35. (NAMI), N.A.o.M.I., *StigmaFree.* htts://*www.nami.org/stigmafree.*

36. Henderson, C. and P.C. Gronholm, *Mental Health Related Stigma as a 'Wicked Problem': The Need to Address Stigma and Consider the Consequences.* Int J Environ Res Public Health, 2018. **15**(6).

37. Henderson, C., S. Evans-Lacko, and G. Thornicroft, *Mental illness stigma, help seeking, and public health programs.* Am J Public Health, 2013. **103**(5): p. 777-80.

38. Yap, M.B., A. Wright, and A.F. Jorm, *The influence of stigma on young people's help-seeking intentions and beliefs about the helpfulness of various sources of help.* Soc Psychiatry Psychiatr Epidemiol, 2011. **46**(12): p. 1257-65.

39. Link, B.G., et al., *Public conceptions of mental illness: labels, causes, dangerousness, and social distance.* Am J Public Health, 1999. **89**(9): p. 1328-33.

40. Kelly, T.M. and D.C. Daley, *Integrated treatment of substance use and psychiatric disorders.* Soc Work Public Health, 2013. **28**(3-4): p. 388-406.

41. Ross, S. and E. Peselow, *Co-occurring psychotic and addictive disorders: neurobiology and diagnosis.* Clin Neuropharmacol, 2012. **35**(5): p. 235-43.

42. Ng, J., C. Sutherland, and M.R. Kolber, *Does evidence support supervised injection sites?* Can Fam Physician, 2017. **63**(11): p. 866.

43. Platt, L., et al., *Needle syringe programmes and opioid substitution therapy for preventing hepatitis C transmission in people who inject drugs.* Cochrane Database Syst Rev, 2017. **9**: p. CD012021.

44. Sawangjit, R., T.M. Khan, and N. Chaiyakunapruk, *Effectiveness of pharmacy-based needle/syringe exchange programme for people who inject drugs: a systematic review and meta-analysis.* Addiction, 2017. **112**(2): p. 236-247.

45. Peiper, N.C., et al., *Fentanyl test strips as an opioid overdose prevention strategy: Findings from a syringe services program in the Southeastern United States.* Int J Drug Policy, 2019. **63**: p. 122-128.

46. Rozsa, M., *Missouri state senator on prescription abuse: "If they overdose and kill themselves, it just removes them from the gene pool".* Salon, March 7, 2017. **https://www.salon.com/2017/03/07/ missouri-state-senator-on-prescription-abuse-if-they-overdose-and-kill-themselves-it-just-removes-them-from-the-gene-pool/**.

CHAPTER ELEVEN

Education and
Prevention Strategies
By Ellen Krohne

Now that you have read and experienced these stories of loss and grief in Part Two, and examined some of the things we can learn from them in Chapter Ten, Diana, Matthew and I feel it is imperative to share with you some reasons for hope. We don't want to leave you with the impression that the opioid crisis has no possible solution.

We know that there are more and more families each day that are experiencing the loss of a loved one due to this crisis. We know there are so many individuals, families, loved ones and friends fighting addiction right now, struggling. We also know there are many smart and dedicated researchers, law enforcement officers, policy makers, educators, and local leaders working to help stem the tide. And, while there is a lot of work ahead, there are already some encouraging trends.

Information and Education

There is a massive amount of information available on opioids, substance abuse and addiction. Anyone wanting to become educated can certainly do so. Some of our grieving families just didn't know where to turn for information. But in today's environment, information is bountiful. To give you a jump-start, below is a list of organizations with websites that contain various pieces of information related to opioids, substance use or addiction. These are some of the resources that I've used in my research for this chapter:

- National Institute on Health (NIH) *www.nih.gov*
- National Institute on Drug Abuse (NIDA) *www.drugabuse.gov*
- Office of National Drug Control Policy (ONDCP) *www.whitehouse.gov/ondcp*
- Substance Abuse and Mental Health Services Administration (SAMHSA) *www.samhsa.gov*
- National Council on Alcoholism and Drug Abuse (NCADA) *www.ncada-stl.org*
- National Education Association (NEA) *www.neatoday.org*
- Community Anti-Drug Coalitions of America (CADCA) *www.cadca.org*
- National Conference on State Legislators (NCSL) *www.ncsl.org*
- Drug Free Communities (DFC) *www.whitehouse.gov/ondcp/grants-programs*
- Center for Disease Control (CDC) *www.cdc.gov/opioids*
- U. S. Department of Health and Human Services (HHS) *www.hhs.gov/opioids*
- Prevention First *www.prevention.org*
- Partnership for Drug Free Kids *www.drugfree.org*

The amount of information may seem a little overwhelming. Certainly, the acronyms are! There is an ever-growing body of information becoming available, and in this chapter we hope to summarize some of the most important issues surrounding education and prevention.

Besides the wealth of information now available, there is good news to be found in the increasingly strong, nationwide focus on the prevention of misuse and addiction, which has developed over the last decade. In the balance of this chapter, I'll focus on prevention strategies, the information every parent should know and the actions they should take, and some things we can all do to help prevent substance use.

Prevention

The goal of substance use prevention is to keep people from misusing drugs, alcohol and tobacco by stopping them before they even start. Never *starting* to use opioids, or other addictive substances, is the best course a person can take to avoid the heartbreak of addiction. Of course, if opioids are prescribed by your physician, I'm not suggesting you shouldn't take them – just be sure to discuss the possible consequences with the physician. Perhaps a better way to say this is that one should never start to use opioids or other drugs that are not prescribed for them, or use prescribed drugs differently than directed by the prescription or physician.

Important lessons are being applied from other successful prevention programs, such as those that were developed to stop smoking, and to encourage seat belt use. According to the Center for Disease Control, adult smoking in the U. S. has been reduced from 40% in the 1970's to 14% in 2017. Seat belt use in the U.S.

has grown from just 14% in 1984 to 90% in 2016, per the National Highway Traffic Safety Administration. While legislation has played a role in these improved statistics, the efforts to educate the public on the consequences of smoking, and the ways in which seat belts save lives, have had a powerful impact as well.

Before we dive into prevention strategies, let's first seek to understand why early prevention is seen as imperative. As defined by the National Institute on Drug Abuse (NIDA), addiction is a chronic, relapsing disorder characterized by compulsive drug seeking and use, despite consequences. It is a brain disorder that may linger for a long time, even well after the person has stopped taking the drugs.

The National Institute on Drug Abuse has a plethora of valuable research and information on its website at *www.drugabuse. gov*. The following paragraphs are a summary of that information:

How does drug addiction work?

Addiction is a lot like other chronic diseases, such as diabetes. Both disrupt the normal, healthy functioning of an organ in the body. If left untreated, both can last a lifetime and may lead to death.

The initial decision to take drugs, including opioids, is typically voluntary, (although this does not take into account the complicated relationships surrounding prescribed drugs). With continued use, self-control becomes impaired. This is the hallmark of addiction. Brain imaging studies of people who are addicted show that changes have occurred in their brain, in areas that include those critical to judgment, decision-making, learning and memory, and behavior control. These changes help explain the compulsive nature of addiction, and why "just stopping" is so difficult.

Why are children and teens more likely to be at risk for poor judgment about drug use?

Brain imaging studies also show that the parts of the brain that control judgment and decision-making do not fully develop until people are in their early or mid-20's. This limits a young person's ability to accurately assess the risks of drug or alcohol experimentation, and makes them more vulnerable to peer pressure as well. Because non-adult brains are still developing, using drugs has more potential to disrupt the brain functions that are critical to motivation, memory, learning, judgment and behavior control. Teens who use alcohol and other drugs often develop family and social problems, poor academic performance, and mental health and other health-related problems.

The NIDA website has an excellent video, "Teen Brain Development," that explains the impact of drugs on an adolescent brain in an easy-to-understand way at: *www.drugabuse.gov/related-topics/addiction-science*.

What other factors are involved in addiction?

Both genetic and environmental factors play a role in how easily a person becomes addicted to drugs. The National Institute on Drug Abuse research indicates that between 40 to 60% of a person's risk for addiction comes from their genetic makeup. Environmental factors include the home environment and parental attitudes, peer influences, and poor school achievement. Teens and people with mental disorders are at a greater risk of drug use and addiction than others. The National Institute on Drug Abuse's research also shows that the earlier a person begins to use drugs or alcohol, the more likely he or she is to develop serious problems, due to the harmful effect that drugs have on the developing brain.

For these reasons, children in elementary, junior high and high schools have long been, and continue to be, the primary focus of prevention measures.

> *"It is easier to stay off drugs*
> *than to get off drugs"*
> — Billboard on Rte. 16, near Hillsboro, Illinois

Substance Use Prevention Strategies

As discussed in Chapter One, earlier decades dealt with drug addiction with different methods than those proposed today. In the '70's and early '80's, drug policies centered on punishment and prohibition, judging that people who were addicted to drugs were simply making poor moral choices. The early prevention programs mirrored this theory. Advances in prevention programming in the last two decades have improved their efficacy by becoming more "evidence-based."

D.A.R.E. – One of the first well-known substance abuse programs. Did it work?

D.A.R.E. (Drug Abuse Resistance Education) is one of the best-recognized and oldest prevention programs. The information below was sourced from D.A.R.E.'s website at *www.dare.org*.

Created in 1983 as a joint effort between the Los Angeles Police Department and the Los Angeles Unified School District, D.A.R.E.'s goal was to "break the generational cycle of drug abuse, related criminal activity, and arrest." Given that few classroom teachers had the knowledge required to deliver a drug abuse prevention program, and given the growing substance abuse rates, D.A.R.E. was welcomed in schools.

The hallmark "Just Say No" program grew rapidly. The course was funded by private donations and by the Drug-Free Schools and Communities Act in 1989. By 2017, over 114 million students across all 50 states had completed the 17-week course. D.A.R.E. was typically taught in the fifth or sixth grade by a trained, uniformed police officer, one hour a week for ten weeks, with little to no cost to the school.

D.A.R.E. was the program given to my children in the 1990's, and I have to say it made an impact on them. They came home with lots of questions and feeling "scared" about drugs. I thought this was a pretty good outcome.

However, in 1998, D.A.R.E. failed to meet the federal requirements for receiving federal grant money, in that it was not "research-based" and had little to no evidence to support its effectiveness, and thus it was excluded from federal funding. Several studies published in the late 1990's indicated that the original D.A.R.E. program had little to no effectiveness in preventing alcohol or drug use.

In response, D.A.R.E. changed their programs to be more focused on decision-making, in order to positively address high-risk situations in a child's life, rather than just teaching abstinence. The newest D.A.R.E. program, "Keeping it REAL," is still delivered by uniformed officers, but is more interactive than the original and has been tested for effectiveness, as are other federally funded programs that deliver similar prevention content.

Other Prevention Programs in Schools Today

Many organizations, including some of the agencies listed as resources above, have prevention programs available for schools today. Some schools deliver prevention programs with trained internal staff, while others hire independent, third-party agencies to deliver these programs. Sometimes they are considered part of health education and sometimes they stand alone. Some programs are started as early as kindergarten and build throughout high school. Others are started in later elementary or middle school grades, and then refreshed in high school.

A successful program is defined as one that is evidence-based, meaning that it has been shown to improve the results of student surveys about their substance use. A program that is taught in 10 to 12% of U.S. schools is Botvin LifeSkills® Training, which is an interactive classroom program that includes discussion and techniques to help children accomplish the following:

- Resist peer pressure
- Challenge common misconceptions about tobacco, alcohol, and other drug use
- Examine their self-image and its effects on their own behavior
- Weigh consequences before making decisions
- Cope with anxiety
- Use verbal and nonverbal assertiveness skills

This is the program used in the local school system in my area, and it is delivered by a local not-for-profit, Hoyleton Youth and Family Services, through a state grant. Kristen Shinn, Director of Community Support Services at Hoyleton Youth and Family

Services, enthusiastically described to me the program and its overall results in the U.S.

Evidence-based research (study details at their website, *www. lifeskillstraining.com/evaluation-studies/*) indicates the following statistics for those enrolled in the LifeSkills® Training program:

- Cuts tobacco use by 87%
- Cuts alcohol use by 60%
- Cuts marijuana use by 75%
- Cuts methamphetamine use by 68%
- Cuts poly-drug use by 66%
- Reduces pack-a-day smoking by 25%
- Decreases use of inhalants, narcotics, and hallucinogens
- Reduces violence
- Reduces risky driving behavior
- Demonstrates effects on HIV-risk behavior

She points out that the program must be tailored to address the issues in each community, and each school within the community, in order to be effective. While alcohol and tobacco are almost always the primary focus of prevention programming, some parts of the country also have a focus on marijuana use, for example. Some areas are heavily impacted by heroin and fentanyl, while others are dealing more with methamphetamines. Programming needs to reflect those differences.

Very different than the scare tactics previously used to teach children about drugs, the programs today are aimed at helping them build skills that can aid them in many areas of their lives, including making decisions about substance use and abuse. Skills and behaviors to help cope with anxiety, and self-image tools that may help children to avoid the development of mental health issues, which can lead to substance abuse, are prevalent themes in all of the programs I reviewed. A comprehensive list of substance abuse prevention programs can be found on the (SAMHSA) Substance Abuse & Mental Health Services Administration website at *www.samhsa.gov*.

Evidence-based prevention programs are helping to make an impact as our youth's addiction rates are trending downward, even though there are other age groups that continue to trend upward. Based on the National Institute on Drug Abuse's website statistics at *www.drugabuse.gov*, for 2018, past-year use of illicit drugs other than marijuana are holding steady at the lowest levels in over two decades - 6.1 percent of 8th graders, 9.6 percent of 10th graders, and 12.4 percent of 12th graders. Among 12th graders, the rate of past-year use of illicit drugs other than marijuana has declined by 30.0 percent in the last five years.

For the past three years, many substances have held steady at the lowest levels of use since the National Institute on Drug Abuse survey's inception (or since the survey began asking about them.) In some cases, use has dropped to lower levels than ever before. Substances at historic low levels of use in 2018 include alcohol, cigarettes, heroin, prescription opioids, MDMA (Ecstasy or Molly), methamphetamine, amphetamines, sedatives, and ketamine.

In addition, both binge drinking (defined as having five or more drinks in a row in the last two weeks) and misuse of prescription opioids (Vicodin and Oxycontin) have dropped dramatically across all grade levels. For 12th graders, binge drinking declined from its peak in 1998 of 31.5% to 2018's level of 13.8%, as depicted on the chart from the SAMHSA website:

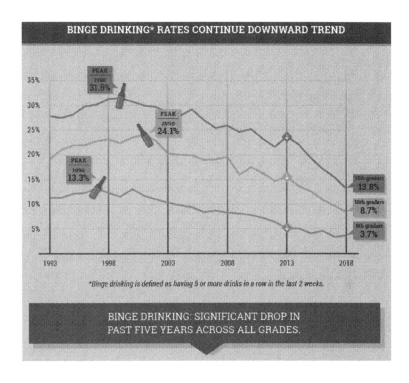

Misuse of Vicodin is down from its peak of 10.5% in 2003 to 1.7% in 2018. Misuse of Oxycontin dropped from 4.5% to 2.3% in that same timeframe, as depicted on the chart from the SAMHSA website:

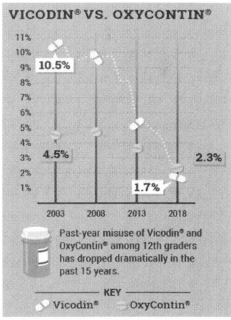

While that progress is such good news, the SAMHSA site also reports that in 2018, heroin use by 12th graders is at 0.4%. That 0.4% means that 13,000 kids are using heroin. In addition, 20% of 12th graders reported that they could get heroin easily if they wanted it, so the situation is still quite serious.

What's Ahead in Prevention Programs?

The National Institute on Drug Abuse, along with many other state and national organizations, is working to improve all phases of drug treatment, including prevention. They have conducted long-term studies that help to point us in the direction of these more effective prevention methods, including:

- Addressing all forms of substance use: prescription drugs, alcohol, tobacco, vaping, and illicit drugs
- Tailoring programs to address specific local problems
- Enhancing family bonding and communication
- Focusing on academic support and social competence skills in school prevention programs
- Repeating prevention techniques; starting the program in the lower grades, and reinforcing it periodically throughout high school
- Employing techniques that include the way children learn and relate, including interactive, open communication, and allowing for the unique circumstances of each child

The D.A.R.E. website also describes some new ways that schools are addressing substance abuse and prevention. Some school districts are determining ways to place more emphasis on helping students with addiction recovery and setting them up for future success, with less emphasis on disciplining them for drug use, thereby treating addiction as the disease it is. Schools are developing programs that help teachers and parents to recognize substance abuse symptoms among students, and to provide information on treatment options. Some schools are introducing online-based prevention programs for both students and parents, thereby overcoming some of the obstacles that are faced in traditional prevention education programs in the classroom.

Prevention programs are also recognizing that the best teachers are often the students themselves. The National Council on Alcoholism and Drug Abuse (NCADA) offers the St. Louis region a host of prevention programming. Their website, *www.ncada-stl.org,* offers excellent information, helpful fact sheets and tips for parents, and programs available for grades K-12. Many of these incorporate student leadership and peer mentors.

Actions to Best Support Youth in Substance Abuse Prevention

So, if you are a parent, or someone who loves a child, what actions can you take to help in the prevention of substance abuse? There are many.

A. *First, educate yourself about the many facets of substance use and prevention.* Gain the knowledge you need to recognize the problem and to advise your children as appropriate. Know what your child is being taught in his or her school's prevention program. Reinforce and support those lessons in your home.

B. *Know the signs that your child may be using drugs, and watch for them.* It's normal for children, especially teens, to sometimes be moody, rebellious, and maybe fickle. They are children, after all, but sometimes it's more than just teenage angst, so be on the lookout.

According to the National Institute on Drug Abuse, the risk of drug use increases greatly during times of transition. For a teenager, such potentially dangerous transitions include moving, a divorce in the family, changing schools, and the death of a loved one. Children may be exposed to substances such as alcohol and prescription or illicit drugs for the first time during their transition from elementary/middle school to high school.

Know the signs that your child is using drugs and act right away. Several of our families' stories include their initial lack of awareness of the problem, and therefore not having acted quickly, as regret points. Some of the common behavioral signs the National Institute on Drug Abuse list are:

- Change in peer group
- Carelessness with grooming
- Decline in academic performance
- Missing classes and skipping school
- Loss of interest in favorite activities
- Trouble at school or with the law
- Changes in eating or sleeping habits
- Deteriorating relationships with family members and friends
- Increased secrecy

From the CDC website, here are some physical symptoms of opioid abuse:

- Slurred speech
- Itching or flushed skin

- Constipation
- Feeling no pain, euphoric or high
- Shallow or slow breathing
- Small pupils
- Lack of energy
- Inability to concentrate
- Nausea or vomiting

A more detailed list of the changes that may indicate substance abuse, (from the NCADA website), is in Appendix D.

One symptom alone may not signal a drug or alcohol problem. Pay attention to your child's patterns of behavior and be alert. Changes may occur over varying periods of time, some subtle and some more obvious. Remember that users are often unaware of their changing behavior and attitudes. In addition to the information above, the NCADA website also has a detailed sheet entitled, "How to Talk to Your Child About Drug Use," which may be helpful to read before having a conversation about suspected drug use.

C. *If you find out that your child is using drugs, take action.* The National Institute on Drug Abuse website at *www.drugabuse. gov* has an in-depth listing of actions and recommendations at "What to Do if Your Young Adult Has a Problem with Drugs." They suggest asking for help from professionals, rather than trying to solve the problem yourself, as the first important step. It takes courage to seek help. There is a lot of hard work ahead, and it may interrupt some of the milestones expected during the teen years. However, treatment can work, and teens can recover from addiction. Treatment enables your child to counteract addiction's powerful, disruptive effects on their brain and behavior, so that they can regain control of their lives. Your quick action can make that possible.

If you need assistance with a child that you suspect may be using drugs, one resource that is available free of charge is the Partnership for Drug-Free Kids. It is a nonprofit organization and has helpline services available via phone, text and email at no cost. Specifically, what they do is to direct you to trusted treatment center locators and resources. They will provide you with resources that include questions to ask treatment providers, advice on insurance and payment, and helpful tips when seeking treatment for a loved one. Their website is: *www.drugfree.org.*

D. *Communicate, Communicate, Communicate!* The NCADA site advises that setting clear, specific "house rules" about alcohol and drug use is a necessary step in preventing underage use. Establish these rules early, and make sure you discuss them as your teen matures. Communicate the consequences for breaking the rules, making sure those consequences are realistic so enforcement is doable.

House rules should be specific, such as not drinking alcohol before age 21; staying clear of ALL drug use, including prescription medicines that aren't your own, and obeying clearly defined curfew rules. Strategies that can assist you to implement house rules include helping your teen find ways to have fun without alcohol, and keeping them active in sports and extra-curricular activities and events. Resist giving alcohol to your teens or allowing them to attend parties where alcohol is served.

Setting a regular schedule of family meetings to discuss and resolve problems is also a recommended practice. Make time for open discussion, asking your child, "What would you do if…" questions. These allow sharing of family values and expectations.

Of course, we have to acknowledge that this is the ideal situation where our teens obey the rules and don't try alcohol or drugs, just as requested. As parents we understand that experimentation is normal for children. Working to create an environment where both parent and teen feel comfortable discussing the need to experiment is imperative to successful prevention of substance use.

I'd be a hypocrite if I didn't add to this section my personal experience. My husband and I communicated clear expectations about our zero tolerance for our children's drug use, which we are grateful were observed, as far as we know. But having both been raised in large, German families, beer drinking was considered quite normal for teens. My husband and I did it, and allowed our children to do it as well. Not to excess, but they drank beer, nonetheless. But with the knowledge that I now have about an adolescent's brain development, and the potential negative effects of alcohol as well as drugs, I will certainly educate our children and discuss with them the dangers of continuing this practice with our grandchildren.

Understand, Control, and Dispose of Prescription Medications

Since 2016, when the Center for Disease Control (CDC) released guidelines for prescribing opioid medications for pain, there have been some beneficial changes. Below are some of the recommendations from the CDC website for prescription medications:

A. If your child is (or you are, for that matter) prescribed a medication, particularly a pain medication, clearly understand all effects, including the risks of potential addiction. Opioid pain medications are still legally prescribed to children. Ask your physician for alternatives to opioids and, if that's not possible, monitor the dosing closely. Discuss with the physician any history of addictive tendencies in your family. Advocate for and protect your child.

B. If an opioid medication is prescribed, secure the prescription and monitor the dosing closely, working with your physician. Do not allow a child to self-medicate.

C. Dispose of any unused medication - not just opioids, but all types of medication. Do not keep unused medication "just in case you need it." Note, I am guilty of this one, too, but have now cleaned house. Medicine cabinets left unlocked have been the source of many instances of drug misuse. Safe disposal containers are available at every county health department, and often there are "give back" days for prescription drugs. Please make using these options a habit.

D. Per the National Conference of State Legislators' website, *www.ncsl.org*, in just the last few years, over half of the states have enacted laws restricting opioid prescriptions to only acute pain treatment (except in specific diagnoses, such as some cancer care and end-of-life treatment.) Fifteen states restrict prescriptions to seven days maximum, with some limiting initial prescriptions to three to four days. Eight states have set requirements for doctors to discuss the risks with a minor and their parent/guardian before prescribing opioids. The website above is searchable, and can help you to learn which laws have been enacted in your state. As Matthew suggests in Chapter Ten, let your state and federal legislators know which laws you think are important for them to pass in order to help stem this crisis.

As I was discussing this book with my son, now 35, he reminded me about our experience with opioids. He had a serious knee injury, followed by surgery, when he was a junior in college. He had the surgery in Chicago, and came home to recuperate that summer, with a big bottle of Oxycontin. I didn't know what that was, or that it had any negative side effects. I just knew the doctor had prescribed them, and he was in horrible pain. I insisted over and over that he take the medication. But he refused. He kept saying, "Mom, just get me ice, get me a Tylenol. I'll be ok, really." We argued for days about his stubbornness in not taking what the doctor had prescribed.

I felt a cold chill up my spine when he told me recently why he had refused the medication. He said, "I knew people that used those pills, Mom, and I knew I didn't want to take them." If I had known, we would have discussed his concerns with his physician and sought guidance about the safe and appropriate use of the medication, and explored non-opioid alternatives, hopefully calming his fears about addiction.

We learn from our children, too.

Get involved. The Role of Community Involvement – What Every One of Us Can Do!

There are federal programs that provide grant funding for drug abuse prevention programming. One that appears to be effective is the Drug-Free Communities (DFC) Support Program, created by the Drug-Free Communities Act of 1997. As one of our nation's leading efforts to mobilize local communities for this purpose, it provides grants to community coalitions which work to help reduce substance use among local youth. In the United States there are 3,142 counties (or geographic equivalents, like parishes, for example.) There were 731 active Drug-Free Community Coalitions in 2018, covering about 19% of the population. The federal funding for these coalitions in 2018 was at its highest in the program's 20-year history, at a $99,000,000 investment. Each coalition must provide a one-to-one match for federal dollars. The information on Drug-Free Community Coalitions is at *www.whitehouse.gov/ondcp/grants-programs/.*

Each Drug-Free Community Coalition incorporates a broad cross-section of the community, including parents, youth, business, media, schools, youth-serving organizations, law enforcement, civic organizations, religious organizations, healthcare professionals, state and local governments, and substance abuse organizations. The coalition conducts community assessment surveys and uses this data to develop and implement locally based prevention strategies. These are broad initiatives aimed at addressing and involving the entire community in helping to reduce substance use among youth aged 12 to 17. Eighty-seven percent of DFC Coalitions are targeting opioids, reflecting the ongoing national crisis.

Results have been encouraging. Declines in all four areas of substance abuse focus, in both middle school and high school, have occurred in the communities of DFC Grant Award Recipients since the inception of their programs. Prescription drug misuse has been reduced by 18% among their high school students.

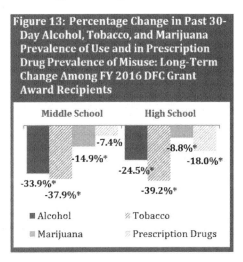

Figure 13: Percentage Change in Past 30-Day Alcohol, Tobacco, and Marijuana Prevalence of Use and in Prescription Drug Prevalence of Misuse: Long-Term Change Among FY 2016 DFC Grant Award Recipients

This table was taken from the 2017 Drug-Free Community National Evaluation End-of-Year Report.

A letter on their website from the overall National Task Force Co-Chairs, Judge Gary Moore from Boone County, Kentucky, and Mayor Mark Stodola from Little Rock, Arkansas, made me hopeful that these coalitions may play a key role in solving the opioid crisis and in reducing the stigma associated with addiction. They said, in part, "We confront the tragedies of this epidemic in rural counties and in urban cities and no portion of society is immune from the devastation. Families are shattered without regard to income, race, ethnicity, gender, educational attainment or family structure."

They continue by describing the action areas. "These recommendations reflect several core convictions: that addiction is an illness, that although law enforcement is critical to an effective response to the epidemic, we cannot simply arrest our way out of a crisis of addiction; to stem the tide of this epidemic and combat the stigma that often accompanies it, we must build partnerships across our communities…"

The five recommendations from the leaders of the coalition sound fairly simplistic, but in reality, they are very hard to implement. The programs are aimed at showing the youth who are at risk for substance use that most of our nation's youth choose *not* to use these addictive substances. The objectives include:

1. Set the tone in the local conversation on opioids
2. Convene community leaders
3. Foster regional cooperation
4. Educate and advocate to state and federal partners
5. Ensure progress for all in formulating responses to addiction

At the meeting sponsored by the Washington County Health Department in January, 2018 on the opioid crisis (the meeting that started all of my worry, research and writing about the opioid crisis), I learned that there is an active coalition in my county. We partner with our neighbors in adjacent Randolph County. Dennis Trask, Youth Prevention Coordinator for the Human Service Center in Red Bud, IL leads the local efforts. I met with him to learn how they are implementing the five recommendations.

The members of this coalition include a robust cross-section of the 12 groups named above, with nearly 300 volunteers involved in some type of coalition work. They meet the third Wednesday of each month. The focus for this alliance has been alcohol use by teens, as their survey and key leader interviews show that to be the primary issue for teens in our two-county region. Fortunately, there is not currently much marijuana or opioid use by teens in the region. However, teens that use alcohol do have a higher likelihood of eventually using opioids and other illegal drugs than those that don't, so the data suggests there will be a strong tie to reductions in other drug usage, too.

I was impressed by how positive and hopeful he was that the coalition, the Southern Illinois Substance Abuse Alliance (SISAA), can make, and is making, a difference. In the last two years, the number of 10th graders who had used alcohol within the previous 30 days has decreased by 3%. This is a small improvement, but a significant one.

Their programming includes:

a. Prevention programs in both counties' elementary and high schools. While some local schools implement the Botvin program discussed earlier, Randolph County uses the similar "Too Good for Drugs" program in Junior High School, and the "Toward No Drugs" in High School. Thirty peer leaders and youth helpers have been trained and utilized across the programs.

b. Introducing the PAX Good Behavior Game, which increases social and emotional skills, to local schools through an additional foundation grant.

c. Facilitation of the Narcan administration training, which is provided to educators, healthcare providers, first responders, law enforcement, and others.

d. Educational information is sent directly to parents and placed in advertisements in local papers (yes, we still have them in Southern Illinois.) Social media strategies were developed to educate everyone on substance abuse, and the strategies which help prevent drug and alcohol use. Their Facebook page lists all of the local events and activities, plus information on substance use prevention.

e. A Speakers Bureau of coalition members is busy making presentations to local organizations regarding the facts of drug misuse and substance abuse prevention strategies, raising general awareness and calling more to action.

f. Participation in the Community Anti-Drug Coalition of America (CADCA), a not-for-profit organization whose mission is to strengthen community coalitions and maintain drug-free communities. CADCA provides public policy advocacy, media and marketing strategies, and training to community coalitions, such as the SISAA. You can learn more about this organization at *www.cadca.org*.

g. Participation in local health fairs and prevention activities, such as the National Prevention Week each May.

h. Access to the "Hidden in Plain Sight" bedroom for parents, so they can learn where to look in their child's room for drugs.

i. Helping to collect over 800 lbs. of prescription drugs to date.

j. Sponsoring six high school students who will go to a substance abuse leadership program this summer. The attendees from last year's program have successfully implemented their plan to create heartening messages for their peers and encouraging them to talk with trusted adults when they need help. The goal this year is to build on that program.

These efforts can help stem the tide. Certainly, doing nothing will only allow the tide to grow ever stronger.

I detail the efforts in my region, not so that you know what we are doing, but rather so that you know what's possible. These efforts may not be appropriate for an urban, less rural setting. Each coalition must design programming that will work for their region. You know what's in the solution set now, so get involved with your local coalition. If you find there isn't a local coalition in your region of your state, contact the Health and Human Services Department, or a local judge or law enforcement official, and get one started. Let's increase the amount of the population covered by a local substance abuse coalition from 19% to 100%. We can combat this epidemic one community, one family, one life at a time. You **can** make a difference.

Benjamin Franklin coined the phrase, "An ounce of prevention is worth a pound of cure." He was referencing fire safety in 1736, but it applies as well to the opioid crisis of today. A SAMHSA cost-benefit analysis indicates that for each dollar invested in effective, local, school-based prevention programming, $18.00 in treatment and other health-care costs can be saved. I hope this chapter has provided you with an understanding of how we can each contribute to drug abuse prevention, and given you some ideas of actions you can take to help stem this crisis.

CHAPTER TWELVE

Concluding Thoughts
By Diana Cuddeback

Thank you for sharing in our stories and thoughts on the opioid crisis, addiction, and grief. This final chapter will look back through the book at the key points concerning grief, and add a few extra ideas about the subject. After years of sitting in sessions and in groups with individuals, couples, and families that are grieving an addiction-related loss, I have come to believe that the painful effect of stigma is one of the most powerful byproducts of death after addiction. Remember, too, that most, though not all, who deal with addiction loss come to the experience after a protracted time of fighting the addiction itself. They come to the actual grief-due-to-death experience tired, drained, and often isolated by years of fighting addiction. They have heard the opinions that their addicted loved one was unworthy, less-than, "scum," or whatever the direct comments have been. They also have heard or felt the indirect comments and attitudes from those around them.

More often than those who grieve the deaths of non-addicted loved ones, people who have lived with addiction loss come to their grief in isolation. They have often dropped, or have been dropped, from the social map. Addiction takes its toll. People just don't know what to say after a while. They grow weary of the difficult stories. It hurts to be around someone in pain, so people move away. People dealing with addiction and then addiction-related death feel the isolation directly or through the silence of unoffered invitations, or phone calls never made.

How are you? Fine. Isn't that the answer most of us want to give and get?

That is not the answer you have to give during the addiction of a loved one. It is not the answer you have after a loss. I want to echo what my two co-authors have highlighted. The stigma of loss from the outside world makes addiction worse, and it makes grief worse. Recognize also that a person supporting someone who is addicted often has her or his own internal stigma about addiction. They have to manage this personal stigma the whole time they are helping their loved one. They have to deal with their personal stigma after that person succumbs to their addiction as well.

There is often a sense of guilt and shame towards themselves as well as their loved one. They ask themselves what else they could have done to prevent the death. They feel alone, they blame themselves as well as the person lost. They hear from the outside world that they were a bad parent, spouse, sibling, friend. And they tell themselves that they did not know enough, do enough, or love enough. Many grieving people deal with guilt, but for this population of grievers, guilt is often louder and stronger. It repeats a soul-crushing litany of could-haves and should-haves.

The idea of disenfranchised grief flows right out of the reality of stigma. Remember, this sort of grief is grief not openly acknowledged, socially sanctioned, or publicly mourned. It is often grief not deemed worthy to be grieved. And, often, it is also grief complicated by trauma - the trauma of deeply disturbing events, and/or trauma from a nervous system chronically on heightened alert. Through examples associated with each story, ideas about managing stigma, disenfranchised grief and traumatic grief have been described in the chapters of this book. Other ideas and suggestions have been shared. This book is just a start. Get curious. Dig deeper. Talk to people. Seek community.

To wrap up the grief section of this book, a few more grief management ideas might be useful.

A wise radiation oncologist in San Marcos, Texas, Dr. David Jones, shared the idea of **The Rule of 60%** years ago. This rule says that when you are 60% done with something, you leave. He was talking about someone in cancer treatment, but it applies beautifully to grieving people too. When you are grieving, your energy, and sometimes your tolerance, is in short supply. As you begin to go back out into the world, you need to go for short periods. If you go and stay until you are 100% ready to leave (or until you feel it is socially appropriate to go), you still have to say goodbye and get out the door. This can leave you exhausted for days, and reluctant to try going out again. If you leave at 60% ready to go, or at 60% of what you feel is socially appropriate, you will have a bit of energy to spare for the goodbyes. You also may not need days to recover from the experience.

Understand, too, that some situations or some people will have you reaching your 60% level more quickly than others. People managing grief and life need to learn to dose themselves with activity and socializing. You add more as you practice and as time goes on, but you carefully control your dose. Control your dose of difficult people, too. Drive your own car. Warn people that you won't be staying for an entire event. Have a friend who can make your goodbyes or run interference. Having a "grief wingman" is helpful. Listen to what your body, heart and mind are telling you. Apply the Rule of 60% and leave. Conserve your energy for you.

Why conserve your energy? Because **grieving takes energy.** It takes incredible energy to manage the pain of grieving while you are living. Grief may have you sitting in one place for hours or cleaning your house with no breaks. Grieving sucks up mental and emotional bandwidth so that accomplishing basic tasks takes a huge effort. Grief seems to be a 24/7 activity running in both the foreground and the background of a grieving person's brain. It is hard to feel rested when you are grieving, because even if you are not actively thinking about grief, the grief is still there at some level.

Conserving your energy is a part of a grieving person's **advocacy for their right to grieve in their way, on their own schedule.** Advocating for yourself as a grieving person is a critical part of managing your grief process. Advocating for yourself includes expressing or not expressing your grief in the ways that work for you. It means finding your own comfort mechanisms. It means going on your own time schedule. Advocating for your own grief means learning what works for you as a grieving person. Learning about grief is critical.

Don't ask for orange juice from an apple. As a grieving person, you will have people in your world that you assume will be there for you, and your pain will be increased by their inability to provide you the support you need. Not everyone can be a companion to someone managing the pain of addiction or grieving a loss. Some people can sit and listen to your pain over and over; others cannot. Some people will mow your lawn, make you meals and get groceries, but they can't sit with you and share stories. The sooner you honestly recognize who can support you and in what ways, the better off you will be. Don't ask for orange juice from an apple. Don't ask an errand runner to sit with you while you cry. If you use your energy expecting, asking for, and being upset from not getting support from people whom you expected to be there for you, you are wasting your energy. It will make your grief process harder. It may not be fair, or right, or even humane, but it is. And remember, grieving takes energy. You need to conserve your energy, so don't waste it squeezing an apple for orange juice.

Learning about grief is important. Those who find themselves grieving for the first time, may come to grief with very limited experience and few coping strategies. Figuring out who in your support network can listen and who likes to be a doer, is important - think orange juice and apple juice here. Finding **professional support** can make a big difference, too. A professional counselor who has a specific expertise in grief can be a great help. Ask what specialized training and what real experience a therapist has in grief work. Don't assume that a counselor really knows grief just because she or he has a degree and a license. Look for grief training, trauma training, and an EMDR (Eye Movement Desensitization and Reprocessing) specialty, among therapy specializations. Ask for referrals from people who deal with grief regularly or have used a therapist themselves. Remember that you are the customer, and you need to feel that you have a good fit with your therapist.

Finding a community of people who are grieving is another important support. This book had its genesis in a grief support group for people with an addiction-related loss. Find a place where your personality and grief style fits. **Give it three** is a good rule of thumb for group support attendance. Going to a group for the first time is never comfortable, but after three sessions you should have some sense of whether or not a group is right for you. See our Resource Section for group connections.

Finally, if you remember nothing else, remember this: **Closure is a myth**. Closure is something television reporters and radio therapists talk about. The idea that you can close off grief is unhelpful. And to grieving people, it is insulting. If you ask someone grieving the death of a loved one, they will tell you that they don't want closure. They don't want to stop thinking about the person who died. They want to think of them and remember them with less pain. They want to find a way to maintain a connection and take that person with them in spirit as they move on in their life. But getting to this place is quite a journey. It is the work of grief. And that grief work is the work of a lifetime.

Heart Open

A poem about Heartlinks Grief Center Addiction Loss Support Group

By Lisa Conner

Dedicated to my adorable daughter, Melissa, (Mel) who is now an angel in heaven.

I'm sitting in a meeting and
looking around

So many of us here
with our heads hanging down

It's not because we're embarrassed
or have something to fear
It's because when we look up
we see others so dear

We see tears in their eyes
and tears on their cheeks
Not a person will lie
about feeling so weak

We also have laughter and smiles for each other
Some hugs and some pats
for our sisters and brothers

We giggle, we cry, we laugh and we shake
We make sure we pass around
the desserts that are baked

We talk about hard times
that have really been bad
To the point we start getting
so very, very mad

We talk about good times and
good memories we shared
Then we laugh and we laugh
and think should we dare

Should we dare have a moment
of beautiful bliss

While in our minds something's
saying hiss, hiss, hiss, hiss

This meeting I'm talking about
isn't for everyone
It's a meeting for parents
who lost their loved one

Not an ordinary death
If there is such a thing
But one that we try hard to
find who is to blame

Well friends, let me tell you,
our child didn't die
From a gunshot or murder
but from being high

Drugs were the culprit
that took our dear soul
It tore and it pulled
and made a big hole

So, while at this meeting
when we're sitting around
We feel safe, understood
and no judgment abounds

Heartlinks Addiction Loss Support
is the name of this meeting
When we're here sometimes
we feel like we're taking a beating

We are not, don't you see
We want it to be
Because it helps us to heal
without making any deals

I'm thankful for this place
and the kind folks that are here
Like I mentioned before
they are all very dear

Concluding Thoughts
by Ellen Krohne

Stigma. The word Matthew and Diana both use to describe a reality that complicates the treatment and bereavement of addicts and their families in this opioid epidemic. A concept the joint co-chairs of the National Task Force of the Drug Free Communities Support Program say we must combat. Our beliefs are firmly embedded, and many of us in the United States, myself included before writing this book, may incorrectly view drug addiction as a personal weakness, not as a disease. I've learned so much. I understand now that any of us could be in these families' shoes. Addiction is a disease of the brain and, more than that, it is a learning disorder. Avoiding the use of drugs has to be a learned behavior, and their use is not a personal weakness. I am grateful to my co-authors, Diana and Matthew, for graciously sharing their insights so that we may better understand addiction and loss.

Disenfranchised. The word Diana uses to describe how each of our families felt when they lost their child, as the loss was shrouded in blame and fault. Their grief was not respected because it resulted from the addicted person's "choice." Several families experienced comments that expressed a dismissal of their child's death because the addicted individual was "at fault." My heart hurt as these brave parents shared their journeys of addiction loss. I am grateful to say I have learned so much from them. I hope you have taken them into your heart.

These two concepts, stigma and disenfranchisement, tie together. If we can reduce the stigma associated with addiction and mental health issues, then we can help to stop the disenfranchisement of their loss. That can create a virtuous circle, where less stigma leads to less disenfranchised grief. And it is up to us to start this virtuous circle turning.

Matthew provided specific and imperative actions for us to help end this crisis – both on Capitol Hill, with our legislators, and by supporting treatment. Diana suggests effective, compassionate acts we can take to help those that are grieving a loss resulting from addiction. And we can all choose to sign up to be organ and tissue donors, giving the gift of life. Each of us can become educated about substance use and addiction and support local prevention strategies. Let us all commit to these actions and bring hope to this crisis.

The battle we must win is not just against the drugs, but against the stigma associated with addiction. Every one of us, dear readers, can treat each person on this journey of addiction with kindness, treating them with the respect you would like your loved one treated with in a similar situation.

We can approach those who are grieving with our hearts open, seeking to help those who are heartbroken. When we do, we courageously start the wheel turning to remove the stigma of addiction, and the disenfranchisement within the grief from addiction loss, and we give honor to those that have lost a loved one to this crisis.

Let us start today.

Thank You for Reading

Dear Reader,

I hope you embraced the families and the information in *Heartbroken – Grief and Hope Inside the Opioid Crisis* and learned as much as I did.

When Diana, Matthew and I wrote this book, our intention was to tell real stories that could give a voice to opioid addiction and loss. To call our readers to action to help stop the stigma associated with addiction and help change the tide of this crisis. We hope you will join us in these efforts.

Another call we ask of you, if you have time, is to provide a review on Amazon. Loved it, hated it – we'd like to hear your feedback. Reviews are what drive people to see the book and will, we hope, have more people, especially parents, taking action. And, will help provide funding for Heartlinks Grief Center, to aid those grieving a loss.

Here's how to find my author page for Heartbroken to leave you review: www.amazon.com/Ellen-Krohne.

Thank you for reading this book, and for your consideration.

Ellen Krohne

Appendices A - I

List of Opioids

In 1970, the United States passed the Controlled Substances Act, a federal policy aimed to improve and regulate the manufacturing, distribution and dispensing of controlled substances. Controlled substances are those drugs or medications that are considered to have some form of abuse potential, and based on that abuse potential, along with the medical value of the drug, these substances are categorized into five schedules[1]. The following is a list of opioid drugs by their scheduled status.

Schedule I: High abuse potential with NO accepted medical use
Heroin, illicit fentanyl analogues

Schedule II: High abuse potential with accepted medical use
Morphine, codeine, hydrocodone (Vicodin), hydromorphone (Dilaudid), methadone (Dolophine), oxycodone (OxyContin, Percocet,

1 Gabay, M. The Federal Controlled Substances Act: Schedules and pharmacy registration. Hosp Pharm. 2013; 48(6).473-474.

Percodan, Roxicodone), oxymorphone,
prescription fentanyl, meperidine (Demerol),
opium, tapentadol (Nucynta)

Schedule III: Intermediate abuse potential (i.e., less than
Schedule II but more than Schedule IV)
Codeine with acetaminophen/aspirin/ibuprofen,
buprenorphine (Suboxone, Subutex)

Schedule IV: Low-Intermediate potential less than Schedule II
but more than Schedule V
Tramadol

Schedule V: Medications with the least potential for abuse
among controlled substances
Robitussin/cough syrup with codeine

Opioid and Other Substance Abuse Terms to Know

Acute Pain: Pain that usually starts suddenly and has a known cause, like an injury or surgery. It normally gets better as your body heals, and lasts less than three months.

Benzodiazepines: Sometimes called "benzos," these are sedatives often used to treat anxiety, insomnia, and other conditions. Combining benzodiazepines with opioids increases a person's risk of overdose and death.

Chronic pain: Pain that lasts 3 months or more and can be caused by a disease or condition, injury, medical treatment, inflammation, or even an unknown reason.

Drug misuse: The use of prescription drugs without a prescription or in a manner other than as directed by a doctor, including use without a prescription of one's own; use in greater amounts, more often, or longer than told to take a drug; or use in any other way not directed by a doctor.

Drug abuse or addiction: Dependence on a legal or illegal drug or medication. See Opioid use disorder.

Fentanyl: Pharmaceutical fentanyl is a synthetic opioid pain medication, approved for treating severe pain, typically advanced cancer pain. It is 50 to 100 times more potent than morphine. However, illegally made fentanyl is sold through illegal drug markets for its heroin-like effect, and it is often mixed with heroin and/or cocaine as a combination product.

Illicit drugs: The non-medical use of a variety of drugs that are prohibited by law. These drugs can include: amphetamine-type stimulants, marijuana/cannabis, cocaine, heroin and other opioids, synthetic drugs, and MDMA (ecstasy).

Medication-assisted treatment (MAT): Treatment for opioid use disorder combining the use of medications with counseling and behavioral therapies.

Morphine milligram equivalents (MME): The amount of milligrams of morphine an opioid dose is equal to when prescribed. This is how to calculate the total amount of opioids, accounting for differences in opioid drug type and strength.

Naloxone: A prescription drug that can reverse the effects of opioid overdose and can be life-saving if administered in time. The drug is sold under the brand name Narcan or Evzio.

Nonmedical use: Taking drugs, whether obtained by prescription or otherwise, not in the way, for the reasons, or during the time period prescribed. Or the use of prescription drugs by a person for whom the drug was not prescribed.

Non-opioid therapy: Methods of managing chronic pain that do not involve opioids. These methods can include, but are not limited to, acetaminophen (Tylenol®) or ibuprofen (Advil®), cognitive behavioral therapy, physical therapy and exercise, medications for depression or for seizures, or interventional therapies (injections).

Non-pharmacologic therapy: Treatments that do not involve medications, including physical treatments (e.g., exercise therapy, weight loss) and behavioral treatments (e.g., cognitive behavioral therapy).

Opioid: Natural or synthetic chemicals that interact with opioid receptors on nerve cells in the body and brain, and reduce the intensity of pain signals and feelings of pain. This class of drugs includes the illegal drug heroin, synthetic opioids such as fentanyl, and pain medications available legally by prescription, such as oxycodone, hydrocodone, codeine, morphine, and many others. Opioid pain medications are generally safe when taken for a short time and as prescribed by a doctor, but because they produce euphoria in addition to pain relief, they can be misused.

Opioid analgesics: Commonly referred to as prescription opioids, medications that have been used to treat moderate to severe pain in some patients. Categories of opioids for mortality data include:

- Natural opioid analgesics, including morphine and codeine;
- Semi-synthetic opioid analgesics, including drugs such as oxycodone, hydrocodone, hydromorphone, and oxymorphone;
- Methadone, a synthetic opioid;
- Synthetic opioid analgesics other than methadone, including drugs such as tramadol and fentanyl.

Opioid use disorder: A problematic pattern of opioid use that causes significant impairment or distress. A diagnosis is based on specific criteria, such as unsuccessful efforts to cut down or control use, or use resulting in social problems and a failure to fulfill obligations at work, school, or home, among other criteria. Opioid use disorder has also been referred to as "opioid abuse or dependence" or "opioid addiction."

Overdose: Injury to the body (poisoning) that happens when a drug is taken in excessive amounts. An overdose can be fatal or nonfatal.

Physical dependence: Adaptation to a drug that produces symptoms of withdrawal when the drug is stopped.

Prescription drug monitoring programs (PDMPs): State-run electronic databases that track controlled substance prescriptions. PDMPs help providers identify patients at risk of opioid misuse, abuse and/or overdose due to overlapping prescriptions, high dosages, or co-prescribing of opioids with benzodiazepines.

Tolerance: Reduced response to a drug with repeated use.[2]

---

2 Above information courtesy of the CDC.

Resources for Those Seeking Help with Addiction

– Substance Abuse and Mental Health Services Administration (SAMHSA) www.samhsa.gov.

> A link on SAMHSA for a listing by state of opioid and substance abuse treatment centers can be found at https://dpt2.samhsa.gov/treatment/

– National Institute on Health (NIH) www.nih.gov
– National Institute on Mental Health (NIMH) www.nimh.nih.gov
– National Institute on Drug Abuse (NIDA) www.drugabuse.gov
– Office of National Drug Control Policy (ONDCP) www.whitehouse.gov/ondcp
– National Council on Alcoholism and Drug Abuse (NCADA) www.ncada-stl.org
– National Education Association (NEA) www.neatoday.org
– Community Anti-Drug Coalitions of America (CADCA) www.cadca.org

- National Conference on State Legislators (NCSL) www.ncsl.org
- Drug Free Communities (DFC) www.whitehouse.gov/ondcp/grants-programs
- Center for Disease Control (CDC) www.cdc.gov/opioids
- U. S. Department of Health and Human Services (HHS) www.hhs.gov/opioids

   Note: This site provides a listing of all treatment facilities in the U.S. by zip code
- Prevention First www.prevention.org
- Partnership for Drug-Free Kids www.drugfree.org
- Alcoholics Anonymous www.aa.org 24/7 hotline: 303-322-4444
- Narcotics Anonymous www.NA.org 24/7 hotline: 303-832-DRUG

How Can I Tell If My Child is Using Alcohol or Other Drugs?

From the NCADA website at *www.ncada-stl.org*

1. Is he/she becoming more:
   a. Irritable
   b. Uncooperative
   c. Violent
   d. Depressed
   e. Negative

2. Has it become more difficult to communicate with your child? Does your child refuse to talk about:
   a. Alcohol or other drugs
   b. Activities with friends
   c. Negative effects of alcohol and other drugs

3. Does your child show any of these physical symptoms:
   a. Increased sensitivity to smell, touch or taste
   b. Extra large or small pupils of the eyes

    c. Excessive giggling

    d. Disorientation

    e. Red eyes

    f. Excessive coughing

    g. Weight gain or loss

    h. Severe headaches

4. Is she/he becoming less responsible about:

    a. Doing chores

    b. Coming home on time

    c. Personal cleanliness/hygiene

    d. Money

5. Has your child recently:

    a. Stolen money or property

    b. Dropped out of classes or school

    c. Insisted the drugs or alcohol you found were not his or hers

    d. Come home with strange stains on his or her clothing

    e. Changed peer groups, dropped long-time friends

    f. Lost interest in school, sports and other activities

    g. Refused to go to school

    h. Talked about dropping out of school

    i. Started wearing long sleeves

    j. Come home smelling like alcohol or smoke

    k. Asked to consume alcohol in the house

    l. Hidden liquor, wine or beer containers or drugs/paraphernalia in his/her bedroom

Resources for Grief Support

For Children and Families - General Grief:

The National Alliance for Grieving Children (NAGC) is a nonprofit organization that raises awareness about the needs of children and teens who are grieving a death, and provides education and resources for anyone who supports them. *www.childrengrieve.org/*

Grief Support Program Locator- *www.childrengrieve.org/find-support*

Grief Support Resources- *www.childrengrieve.org/resources*

The Dougy Center is a nonprofit organization that provides a safe place for children, teens, young adults and their families who are grieving a death to share their experiences through peer support groups, education, and training. *www.dougy.org/*

Grief Support Program Locator: *www.dougy.org/grief-support-programs/*

Grief Support Resources: *www.dougy.org/grief-resources/*

KidSaid is an online support group resource for kids and teens to help each other deal with grief and loss. There is an email support group, plus places to share writing and art, and a place to ask questions. It is part of the GriefNet website. *www.kidsaid.com/index.html*

For Children and Families - Addiction Grief:

Eluna (formerly Moyer Foundation) supports children and families impacted by grief or addiction. Resources and programs address the needs of children experiencing powerful, overwhelming and confusing emotions associated with the death of someone close to them, or substance abuse in their family. **Camp Mariposa** operates year-round for children dealing with addiction and loss issues. *www. elunanetwork.org/*

Adults (General Grief):

What's Your Grief is a website that promotes grief education, exploration, and expression in both practical and creative ways, including a blog, webinars, eCourses, and written materials. *www.whatsyourgrief.com/*

Compassion Books offers a large selection of books about loss and grief. This website has books for helping people of all ages with many different losses. *www.compassionbooks.com/*

GriefNet is an internet community of persons dealing with grief, death and major loss. There are multiple grief groups available for a variety of losses, as well as resource and research information. *www.griefnet.org/*

GriefNet also has an online email support group for people dealing with child loss due to substance abuse. *www.griefnet. org/support/groups.html*

The Grief Toolbox is a website that compiles resources to address the rigors of managing the loss of a loved one.

With varying artwork and articles that provide interesting perspective, the website is helpful for those struggling with loss. *www.thegrieftoolbox.com/*

GriefLink is a website providing resources, links to support groups and links to individual therapists who specialize in grief. *www.grieflink.com/*

Grief Helps offers a variety of free, on-line resources to support the grieving. You will find information, encouragement and inspiration from blogs, mini-videos and books, photography and more. *www.griefhelps.com/*

Grief Watch offers many products, resources and links for grieving individuals. www.griefwatch.com

Grief Share is a faith-based grief support and information source with free daily emails for grieving individuals. *www.griefshare.org/*

Share Grief is an online resource for grief information and grief support services. *www.sharegrief.com/*

Centering Corporation provides a large selection of grief books, other grief resources and publishes Grief Digest magazine. *www.centering.org/*

Adults (Substance Related):

GRASP is Grief Recovery After Substance Abuse Passing, a national resource founded to provide sources of help, compassion and understanding for those whose loved one died from substance abuse or addiction. They also provide online and in-person support groups throughout the country. Broken No More is a sister site that discusses substance abuse-related issues on Facebook. *www.grasphelp.org/* Facebook page: *https://www.facebook.com/groups/grasphelp*

International Overdose Awareness Day is an annual global event to raise awareness of overdose and reduce the stigma of drug-related deaths. Acknowledging the grief felt by families and friends, Overdose Day spreads the message that the tragedy of overdose is preventable and connects people to a day of support. *www.overdoseday.com/*

Survivors Resources is a non-profit organization that offers support groups, crisis response, grief counseling and other services for families of those who died due to homicide, suicide, accidental overdose or violence. *www.survivor-resources.org/*

Family Interview Questionnaire

Questions for my interviews with families for Book on Opioids and Grief
08/16/18

Name: _____

Loved One: _____

Date: _____

1. Tell me about yourself.

2. Tell me about your family.

3. Tell me about your loved one that died.

4. What are your favorite memories about him/her?

5. What was their life like – happy or not?

6. What did you know about their substance use?

7. Was there something that you think led them to using opioid/ drugs – drivers or motivations for use?

8. How and when did you first learn they were addicted?

9. How did you handle discussing your loved one's addiction – who did you tell, what did you keep private?

10. Did they try and get help or did you/others try to help them?

11. Would you change anything about how you handled this?

12. Do you have any "hard" memories – things you did trying to help your loved one that you thought you would never do?

13. How did your loved one die?

14. How did you learn of their death?

15. What were your first thoughts and feelings on hearing of their death?

16. Tell me about that first day when you found out – what did you do, how did you feel?

17. What do you recall about making the funeral arrangements and services?

18. How did people react when they learned of his/her death?

19. Can you recall for me some acts of kindness or helpful/useful things others did after their death?

20. Did anyone say or do anything that surprised you or was painful for you?

21. What was your last interaction with your loved one before they died?

22. How did you express your grief?

23. What took your mind off the pain of her/him being gone? How did you cope?

24. Did you talk with anyone about how you felt, your grief?

25. Did her/his death change your relationship with anyone?

26. Did her/his death impact your faith?

27. How did her/his death change your life?

28. What would you like to be sure our readers know about your loved one?

29. What would you like to be sure our readers know about losing a loved one to drugs?

30. What advice would you give to others on what to do to help a loved one on drugs?

31. What changes in laws do you think would be helpful to stem the drug crises?

32. What has been the hardest part of all of this?

33. In one word, how would you describe your loss?

Correspondence from Chapter Eight

This is the email I received from David Wheeler in response to my letter requesting permission from Benjamin Wheeler's parents to use his name in the book.

Hello Ellen:

Thank you for the recent package and letter -- we received them the other day.

We are so appreciative that you asked for our permission to mention Ben in your upcoming book -- it is unfortunate that most people who want to include our son in something they're writing or producing are not as gracious or respectful as you are. We are very grateful for your kind request and we'd be honored to have our Benny mentioned in your book, not least because the circumstances by which his name arises are so compelling and give us no small amount of comfort.

This, as you must know, is a very difficult week for us, but we are holding our own and keeping close.

And if it's possible, please convey our warmest and deepest respects to the mom you interviewed in your book -- we wish only the best for her as she, also, navigates this rocky, unwanted path.

Best regards,

David

Discussion Questions for Book Clubs

Discussion Questions on the Families' Opioid Journey:

1. Which of the six stories did you find most difficult to read? What emotion did it evoke in you?

2. What "warning signs" of addiction did some of the parents fail to recognize right away?

3. Some of the parents did difficult things to keep their children alive. Put yourself in their situation; what do you think you would do or not do?

4. Which of the six parents would you most like to meet and talk to? Hug?

5. Share a favorite scene from the families' stories. Why did this stand out?

Discussion Questions on Grief:

6. Have you experienced grief from a traumatic event in your life? If so, how does that compare to the parent's grief from their loss?

7. Diana describes many ways to manage the grief from addiction loss in Grief Reflections, after each story. Discuss grief management techniques that you have used after a loss, and how these may differ from managing grief from addiction loss.

8. If you read my first book, **We Lost Her**, compare how the family coped with their grief in that book with how the families that lost their child coped with their grief in **Heartbroken**.

Discussion Questions on the Opioid Crisis:

9. What new things did you learn about the opioid crisis from **Heartbroken**?

10. Was your opinion of addiction changed by what the authors suggest in this book about the stigma of addiction?

11. The authors suggest several actions we can each take to help stem the opioid crisis. What actions can you commit to, with your family and within your community?

General Discussion Questions

1. What do you want to be sure the adolescents in your life (children, grandchildren, friends) know about opioids and addiction?
2. What prevention programs are available in your schools?
3. In Chapter 11 the authors discuss education and prevention strategies. Is there a substance abuse coalition in your local region? If so, discuss what actions the coalition is taking. If there isn't one, what can be done to start one?
4. What laws are already enacted in your state to deal with opioid prescriptions? What laws could be changed to aid in lessening the availability of opioids, especially to minors?
5. Are there safe-injection sites in your region? If not, what can be done to facilitate the development of a site?
6. Is Narcan available to your local law enforcement, health professionals, schools, etc.? If not, what can be done to ensure Narcan is available?
7. Were you surprised about the ability of those addicted to drugs to be organ donors? What did you learn about the donation process?

8. If you are a parent, what can you do to protect your child from addiction? How has this book informed that answer? What else do you need to know, and where can you find that information?

9. What techniques have you learned about managing grief from addiction loss? Compare grief experiences you have had in your life with those of the parents in the book.

Authors' Bios

Ellen Krohne has been blessed to have had many "acts" in her work life. She worked for Illinois Power Company for 27 years, from front-line customer service to VP of Customer Service; as an international business consultant for a decade; and as Executive Director of the Leadership Council of Southwestern Illinois until her retirement three years ago.

She treasures her bachelor's and master's degrees in organizational management, both earned as an adult while working full time and raising a family. She recently completed a certification in **The Opioid Crisis in America,** a course of study offered by Harvard University. Ellen is currently enjoying being a grandparent, traveling, and doing volunteer work in retirement with her husband, Bill. She feels grateful to have authored her first book, **We Lost Her**, and to have had the honor to tell the families' stories for this book, **Heartbroken: Grief and Hope Inside the Opioid Crisis**. She is looking forward to continuing her writing career as her "next act."

Diana Cuddeback, LCSW is the Founding Director of Heartlinks Grief Center in Belleville, Illinois. Trained as a family therapist, she holds a Master's degree in Social Work from the George Warren Brown School of Social Work at Washington University. Diana has worked in hospice, counseling, and grief therapy since 1991. Diana started Heartlinks, a  program of Family Hospice, in 1997 and, along with the Heartlinks team, has provided innovative programs both within and outside of Heartlinks Grief Center, for diverse populations.

Diana brings extensive trauma-related grief experience, and guides the Addiction Loss Support Group at Heartlinks Grief Center. Her mission is to create a meaningful community of support for grieving people, filled with learning, activity, fun, and connection.

Matthew Ellis earned a Bachelor of Arts in Psychology from Rockhurst University, has a Masters of Psychiatric Epidemiology from Washington University in St. Louis, and is currently a doctoral candidate of Behavioral Science in the College of Public Health and Social Justice at Saint Louis University. Based in St. Louis, at the Washington University  School of Medicine in the Department of Psychiatry, Matthew is an epidemiologist who has worked on the opioid epidemic for over a decade, with an emphasis on transitions to heroin, the impact of abuse-deterrent opioids, and understanding the demand side of opioid use by linking quantitative and qualitative data.

Matthew has published a number of opioid-related research articles and reviews in the *New England Journal of Medicine, JAMA Psychiatry,* and *Drug and Alcohol Dependence,* among others, and has been featured in media outlets such as *VICE* and *Forbes.*

Made in the USA
Monee, IL
03 February 2020